Jesus Christ: A Pagan Myth

About the Authors Laurence E. Dalton is a graduate of the University of Oregon in Portland with a double major in psychology and sociology. During his career he has been an editor of an Air Force newspaper, a social worker, a retail store owner, and author.

Shirley Strutton Dalton graduated from California State University, San Bernardino with an MA in administration and accounting. During her career she was a self-employed Certified Public Accountant and a part-time author. She is currently working on two other books on genealogy, her hobby.

Other Books *Self Publishing POD Companies: BookLocker vs AuthorHouse, iUniverse, Xlibris, Lulu, and BookSurge*, 2008.

Men, Women, and Gods and Other Lectures by Helen H. Gardner, edited by Shirley Strutton Dalton and Laurence E. Dalton, 2001.

Jesus Christ: A Pagan Myth

* * *

Evidence that Jesus Never Existed

Laurence E. Dalton

Shirley Strutton Dalton

Jesus Christ: A Pagan Myth

Evidence that Jesus Never Existed

Published by:
CreateSpace
CreateSpace.com

ISBN 13: 978-1440449338

Printed in the United States of America

In Memory, Fay Marie
For everything there is a season,
And a time for every matter under heaven:
A time to be born, and a time to die . . .
a time to weep, and a time to laugh;
a time to mourn, and a time to dance . . .
Ecclesiastes 3:1-2,4

Contents

Part I

Commentary on Mark

Chapter 1

Birth, Baptism and Ministry

Seeking to kill the future emperor Augustus, the Roman Senate issued an order to have all Roman male infants killed.
– Authors

Was Jesus Jewish? Pagan? Did he exist, and if not, who created the myth of Jesus? Liberals, skeptics and even atheists often accept as valid certain assumptions such as the existence of Jesus and his Jewishness.

Part I of this book is a critical commentary on the earliest gospel, Mark, and will show that his Jesus is a literary fiction, and a Greco-Roman one at that, not Jewish.

Part II of this book searches for answers to questions such as these:

- Did Paul have any knowledge of Jesus or Peter?

- Did Paul know about Jesus' Last Supper or about his resurrection appearances?

- Was Paul a Jew, a pagan, or a Christian?

- Did he create Jesus, and if he did not, who did?

- Who founded Christianity?

A Note on Terminology

In this book, what Christians call the Old Testament (OT), we will call the Jewish Scriptures (hereafter JS); the New Testament will be called the Christian Scriptures (hereafter CS). No one knows who wrote the four gospels, but we will for convenience accept Mark (Mk), Matthew (Mt), Luke (Lk), and John (Jn) as the authors of the canonical gospels. Mk 1.2 will signify Mark Chapter 1, verse 2. We will use BCE (Before the Common Era) instead of BC and CE (the Common Era) instead of AD.

"Gentile" (Greek *ethnos* or *nation*) is used in the *Christian Scriptures* to refer to a non-Jew, that is someone not born of a Jewish mother or one who has not been converted to Judaism."[1] We will replace the word gentile with the word *pagan*, meaning only a person who is neither a Jew nor a Christian.

Most modern commentators on the *Christian Scriptures* use the phrase *Jewish Christian*, though it appears nowhere in the CS. It is as if Jews are still considered a biological race, a concept long ago discredited. Is a Christian who converts to Judaism called a Christian Jew? A Jew who has converted to Christianity, we will designate a Christian of Jewish background.

Although some ancient Jews interpreted the *Jewish Scriptures* symbolically, they nonetheless preserved the literal sense of the text where it was needed. For example, Philo of Alexandria was a Hellenized Jew, i.e., a Jew who was familiar with Greco-Roman culture. This Biblical commentator held that abstaining from pork reminded people not to be enslaved to greed, but he also took the command literally, believing that Jews should observe the law forbidding the eating of pork.

Ancient Christians interpreted the *Jewish Scriptures* symbolically, often destroying any Jewish meaning. For example, in Exodus Moses parts the Red Sea so that the Jewish people escape slavery in Egypt. Many Christians interpreted this passage as predicting that Jesus would save people through baptism.

The *Jewish Scriptures* were completed nearly 200 years before the time of Jesus and all modern commentators, other than literalists, recognize that these scriptures never refer to Christian

---

[1]Cohn-Sherbok, Dan, *A Dictionary of Judaism and Christianity* (Philadelphia: Trinity Press International, 1991), 55.

baptism or any other aspect of Christianity.

The Birth of Jesus

Before turning to our commentary on Mark, we will critically examine the birth stories written about Jesus. According to Matthew and Luke, the father of Jesus was Joseph. Although Mark wrote his gospel about 70 CE, well before Matthew and Luke wrote theirs, he does not know the name of the father of Jesus. Mark knows nothing of any divine and virginal conception of Jesus, his birth in Bethlehem under Herod the Great (36-4 BCE), nor of Jesus' aristocratic ancestry (Mt 1.1-16; Lk 3.23-38).

Pagan divine men were often depicted as having a noble and divine heritage. The philosopher, Pythagoras (fl 530 BCE), was said to have been descended from noble ancestors and from Apollo, the Greek sun god.[2] The editors of Hellenistic Commentary to the New Testament (hereafter HCNT) point out that Diogenes Laertius (3rd cent. CE) characterized "Plato as the supernaturally conceived son of the god Apollo."[3] Plutarch relates that Alexander the Great was a descendant of the divine Hercules.[4] The gens (tribes) of the Roman kings and rulers of the Republic were also thought of as divine.

Let us compare Jesus with Octavius, the future Emperor Augustus (ruled 27 BCE to 14 CE), as he was a contemporary of Jesus (ca 4 BCE–ca 30 CE). In Matthew, Joseph has a dream in which an angel tells him that "... the child [Jesus] conceived in [Mary] is from the Holy Spirit" (Mt 1.20). Plutarch says that, "[Dreams are] ... a most ancient and respected form of divination ...."[5] (cf. Mt 1.18-2.23). He also says that birds can become

---

[2]Cartlidge, David R. and David L. Dungan, *Documents for the Study of the Gospels* (Philadelphia: Fortress Press, 1980), 134.

[3]Boring, M. Eugene, Klaus Berger, Carsten Colpe, Eds., *Hellenistic Commentary to the New Testament* (Nashville: Abingdon Press, 1995), 33, #1, Plutarch, Lives of Eminent Philosophers, "Plato" 3.1-2,45.

[4]Boring, M., HCNT, 37, #6, Plutarch, Parallel Lives, "Life of Alexander" 2.1-3.2.

[5]Boring, M., HCNT, 40, #9, Plutarch, Moralia, "Dinner of the Seven Wise Men" 159A; "On Inoffensive Self-Praise" 589D.

pregnant by means of a wind.[6] In Greek, *pneuma*, or wind, can mean spirit (cf. Mt 1.18-25). Matthew quotes Isa 7.14, "Look, the virgin shall conceive and bear a son ... " an error perpetuated by Christians to this day since Isaiah actually says *young woman*, not *virgin*.

Suetonius writes that a serpent approached the mother of Augustus, Attia, as she slept in the temple of Apollo and impregnated her.[7]

In Luke's gospel, the angel Gabriel declares to Mary that her child "will be great, and will be called the Son of the Most High, and the Lord God will give to him the throne of his ancestor [King] David. He will reign over the house of Jacob forever, and of his kingdom there will be no end" (Lk 1.32-33). Plutarch relates that before the birth of the Emperor Augustus, a "prediction was made that a citizen of that town (Velitrae) would one day rule the world."[8]

In the ancient pagan world it was common for various gods and rulers to attempt to prevent the birth of a demigod or, failing that, to attempt to kill him shortly after his birth. One of the most popular demigods of the ancient Greek and Roman world was Hercules.[9] In one tradition, Zeus impregnates Alkmene, the mortal woman who was the mother of Hercules. Zeus announces to all the gods that he will make the child who is born on a specific day the king of Perseus' descendants. Hera stops the labor pains of Alkmene so that Hercules is born one day after the date chosen by Zeus; eventually a compromise is worked out and Hercules survives to become king.

In Genesis, the Pharaoh attempts to kill the infant Moses by slaughtering all Hebrew baby boys, but Moses' mother saves her son by sending him down the Nile in a basket. He is rescued and raised by the Pharaoh's daughter. In Matthew's Gospel an angel warns Joseph in a dream and he and Mary flee wit the infant Jesus to Egypt (Mt 2.14-15). To prevent Octavius from be-

---

[6]Boring, M., HCNT, 38, #7, Plutarch "Table Talk" 8.1-3.

[7]Martin, Francis. Ed., *Narrative Parallels to the New Testament* (Society of Biblical Literature. Atlanta: Scholars Press, 1988), 160, Suetonius Augustus 94.

[8]Martin, F., 160.

[9]Philostratus, *The Life of Apollonius of Tyana*. Trans. F. C. Conybeare (Loeb Classical Library. Vol I. 1912. Harvard University Press, 1989), 15.

coming king of the Roman people, "the senate in consternation decree(ed) that no male child born that year should be reared."ix Octavius lived to become Emperor because of the resistance of Roman mothers. At Mt 2.16, Herod the Great attempts to kill Jesus by ordering the death of all babies in and around Bethlehem. There is no evidence of any such slaughter in first-century Judea.

The similarities in the birth stories of Moses, Augustus and Jesus include:

- The birth of all three is predicted;

- Powerful people attempt to kill the newborn hero;

- Each grows up to be a law giver who inaugurates a new age. In addition, Jesus and Augustus each had a divine father and a human mother, and miraculous signs and portents accompany their births as well as their deaths.

The striking similarity between the lives of Jesus and the Emperor Augustus can be seen even more clearly in a resolution passed by the Provincial Assembly of Asia Minor during the reign of Augustus. Among other things, it states that Providence has given

> ...to us Augustus Caesar whom it filled with virtue (arete) for the welfare of mankind, and who, being sent to us and to our descendants as a savior (soter), ... having become visible (phaneis...) ...surpassing all the benefactors ...the birthday of the God (viz., Caesar Augustus) has been for the whole world the beginning of the gospel (evangelion) concerning him, (therefore, let all reckon a new era beginning from the date of his birth...)[10] (Cartlidge's ital.)

According to the Christian Scriptures, the good news or gospel (evangelion) is preached by Jesus. His divinity becomes visible, i.e., he takes on flesh. He has come to benefit the world; he surpasses all others and inaugurates a new age.

---

[10]Cartlidge, D., 13-14.

Problems: Birth Stories in Matthew and Luke

According to Mark, Jesus was apparently born and raised in Galilee, although Matthew relates that Joseph and his wife, Mary, lived in Bethlehem near Jerusalem in Judea and Jesus was born there, not in Galilee.

Matthew says that a widespread belief in the coming of the Messiah, or a king of Israel, existed among Jews of that time. (Matthew equates the two, Mt 2.2,4). King Herod (d 4 BCE) and "all Jerusalem" fear that the "King of the Jews" has been born (Mt 2.3). James H. Charlesworth is correct when he says that most Jews did not expect "the Messiah."[11] The *Jewish Scriptures* do not mention the coming of "the Messiah." Josephus, the Jewish historian, and the Jewish exegete, Philo of Alexandria, both of the first century CE, did not know about the coming of a Messiah or king, nor does the Mishnah (published ca 200 CE).

Luke, as in Mark, has Jesus' parents reside in Nazareth in Galilee, not in Bethlehem as Matthew does. Luke relates that the Emperor Augustus ordered a census to be taken under Quirinius, the governor of Syria (Lk 1.2.) Luke says that all people traveled to their ancestral home towns to be registered (Lk 1.3).

E.P. Sanders, in *The Historical Figure of Jesus*,[12] discusses some problems connected with this census: 1) Quirinius was not Legate of Syria when Jesus was born, but took office in 6 CE, ten or eleven years after Jesus' birth in about 4 or 5 BCE. 2) "Rome... [took] a census of people who lived in Judea, Samaria, and Idumaea — not Galilee,"[13] as it was not a Roman province at that time. Moreover, the idea that people returned to their ancestral home towns for the census is impossible. Chaos would result. The census was done for tax purposes[14] and the Roman imperial government was not concerned with where one's ancestors lived 42 generations before.

Luke identifies Bethlehem in Judea as the city of David (Lk 2.4). It is true that the *Jewish Scriptures* state that David was

---

[11]Charlesworth, James H. "From Messianology to Christology: Problems and Prospects" in Charlesworth, James H., Ed., *The Messiah: Developments in Earliest Judaism and Christianity* (Minneapolis: Fortress Press, 1992), 5.

[12]Sanders, E.P., *The Historical Figure of Jesus* (Penguin USA. 1996), 86-87.

[13]Ibid.

[14]Ibid.

born in Bethlehem and later anointed king there, but, as S. Lachs informs us, Jerusalem is the city of David, not Bethlehem.[15] (See 2 Sam 5.7,9; 2 Sam 6.10,12,16; 1 Chr 11.5,7; 2 Kgs 9.28, 12.22.)[16] David conquered Jerusalem, named it, built part of it (2 Sam 5.7,9), and made it the capital of Israel. The city is even described as the city of David in 2 Sam 6.12: he "went and brought up the ark of God ...to the city of David [Jerusalem]...."[17] The idea that Bethlehem is the city of David is a Christian invention, as is the belief that "the Messiah" would be born there.[18]

Luke says that in the fifteenth year of Tiberius (ca 28/29 CE) Jesus was about 30 years old (Lk 3.1,23). Counting backwards, we arrive at 2 BCE as Jesus' birth year, two years *after* King Herod dies. The trouble is that both Luke and Matthew relate that Jesus was born *before* the king's death in 4 BCE.

Commentary on Mark

The Gospels of Matthew (written ca 80 CE) and Luke (written ca 85 CE) are dependent on Mark which was written ca 70 CE. Thus, Matthew and Luke will not be given much weight where they disagree with Mark. In addition, we will rarely refer to the Gospel of John (written ca 100 CE) since most critical scholars consider this late gospel historically worthless.

We will generally not be concerned with Jesus' teachings but only with the alleged events of his life (such as his baptism, arrest, trial, crucifixion), and his actions (the choosing of his disciples, his exorcisms, cures, and nature miracles , etc.).

Why this disregard for the teachings of Jesus? E.P. Sanders explains why he did not focus on Jesus' teachings in *Jesus and Judaism*, "...scholars have not and, in my judgment, will not agree on the authenticity of the sayings material, either in whole or in part. There are a few sayings on which there is a wide con-

---

[15]Lachs, Samuel Tobias, *A Rabbinic Commentary on the New Testament: The Gospels of Matthew, Mark and Luke* (Hoboken, N.J.: KTAV Publishing House, Inc., 1987), 29.

[16]Ibid.

[17]Ibid., 30, n 8.

[18]Wigoder, Geoffrey, Ed. in Chief, *Encyclopedia of Judaism*, (New York: Macmillan Publishing Co., 1989), 191.

sensus, but hardly enough to allow a full depiction of Jesus."[19]

In our commentary, we will search Mark for answers to questions such as the following:

- Was Jesus familiar with the religious thought and practice of Judaism in the first century CE?

- Was the Marcan Jesus so anti-Jewish as to preclude a Jewish milieu for the gospel? For example, would a Jewish prophet teach contempt for Jewish law?

- Are the accounts of Jesus' life and death derived from the *Jewish Scriptures*?

- How much of Jesus' life is a product of the early church? Has the early church attributed acts and teachings to Jesus in order to provide scriptural support for certain beliefs and practices of the early church, e.g., baptism and the Eucharist?

- Is Mark historically plausible? For example, would the Sanhedrin, the supreme Jewish legal authority in Judea, meet in the darkness of the Passover night to put Jesus on trial?

- Does Jesus fit better in a Jewish or a pagan matrix? Virtually all serious scholars believe that Mark's account of a Jewish Jesus was Hellenized. Is this true, or is Jesus a pagan figure with Jewish dress? In other words, was Jesus a pagan Christ or a Jewish Messiah?

The Good News Gospel: Mk 1.1

"The beginning of the good news of Jesus Christ, the Son of God" is the first verse of the gospel of Mark; it may originally have been a title. It is an incomplete sentence, untypical of Mark', and it is missing from some important early manuscripts.

Only Mark refers to his narrative as the *gospel* or *good news* (Greek *evangelion*), a word found in surviving pagan inscriptions.[20] One from Pirene (9 BCE) in Asia minor is cited in the

---

[19]Sanders, E.P., *Jesus and Judaism* (1985. Philadelphia: Fortress Press, 1989), 4.

[20]Boring, M., HCNT, 169.

Hellenistic Commentary of the New Testament: "...the birthday of the god Augustus was the beginning for the world of the good tidings (*evangelion*)...."[21] (Boring's ital.)

The Epicurean Lucretius (d 55 BCE) says of his teacher:

> Of his revelations — he was a god,
> A god indeed who first discovered
> That rule of life that now is called philosophy;
> ...[his] gospel [was...,
> Broadcast throughout the length and breadth of empires....[22]

John the Baptist

Mark thinks the *Jewish Scriptures* predict that John the Baptist will "Prepare the way of the Lord [Jesus]" (Mk 1.3), attributing the citation to the "prophet Isaiah" though it seems to be a fusion of Mal 3.1 and Isa 40.3.[23] Matthew and Luke fix this by omitting the Malachi cite. Malachi writes that the messenger is to prepare the way for "the Lord of Hosts" (Mal 3.1), and Isaiah tells the King to prepare "a highway for our God" (Isa 40.3). *Lord* is the most frequently used title for God in the *Jewish Scriptures*. The *NRSV Exhaustive Concordance* informs us that the word *Lord* is used to refer to God more than 8,000 times in about 7,000 places.[24] N. Beck writes, "Jesus is by implication 'the Lord' whose way is prepared by John the Baptist."[25] Early Christians saw Jesus as divine; an impossibility if one assumes that Christianity derives from the strictly monotheistic religion of Judaism.

John the Baptist's camel's hair clothing, leather belt, and his diet of locusts and wild honey (Mk 1.6) are based on 2 Kgs 1.8 and Zch 13.4. The Baptist preaches in the wilderness "proclaiming a baptism of repentance for the forgiveness of sins" (Mk 1.4).

---

[21]Boring, M., HCNT, 169, #225.

[22]Boring, M., HCNT, 170, #226.

[23]Lachs, S., *Commentary*, 37.

[24]Metzger, Bruce M., Ed., *NRSV Exhaustive Concordance* (Nashville: Thomas Nelson Publishers, 1991), 772.

[25]Beck, Norman A., *Mature Christianity in the 21st Century: The Recognition and Repudiation of the Anti-Jewish Polemic of the New Testament* (Crossroad Publishing Co. 1994), 140-141.

Matthew deletes "forgiveness of sins"[26] as the status of Jesus has risen and he has no sins that need to be forgiven (cf. Mk 2.5-7,10). Besides, Jesus can forgive sins but a Jewish prophet cannot.

The church became embarrassed by John's baptism of Jesus because the Jewish prophet came to be thought of as spiritually inferior to Jesus. Thus the church altered the text of Mark, forcing John to acknowledge the superiority of Jesus. The Baptist says that "the one to come" will be greater and more powerful than him. The Baptist is unworthy to untie his sandals and he (John) baptizes with water, but the one to come "will baptize with the Holy Spirit" (Mk 1.7-8), though in the gospels Jesus never baptizes anyone, either with water or with the Holy Spirit.

The Baptist and Jesus are non-Jewish when they indicate that baptism can remove sins. In Judaism one who sins must repent, make appropriate restitution, and pray or sacrifice in the temple.[27]

Mark and Matthew relate that "all the people of Jerusalem" and Judea come to the river Jordan, confess their sins and are baptized by John (Mk 1.5; Mt 3.5).

Matthew increases Mark's anti-Judaism when he adds that John rejects many religious leaders (Pharisees and Sadducees) who had come to be baptized, "You brood of vipers! Who warned you to flee from the wrath to come?" (Mt 3.7). In Matthew and Luke, John preaches that those (Jews) who will not accept Jesus will be punished with "unquenchable fire" (Mt 3.12, Lk 3.17, cf. Isa 34.10; 66.24).[28] The Lukan Baptist even condemns the (Jewish) crowds who have come to be baptized, calling them a "brood of vipers" (Lk 3.7). E. Schweizer writes that the poisonous snake metaphor is "vitriolic... [and] used as a term of address is very striking and is almost without parallel...."[29] Almost?

Later (Mk 9.11-13), Jesus says that the Baptist is the resurrected Elijah, the forerunner of the Messiah, but neither the *Jewish Scriptures* nor any first-century Jewish writings assert

---

[26]Lachs, S., *Commentary*, 45.

[27]Cohen, Shaye J. D., Ed., *From the Maccabees to the Mishnah* (1987. Philadelphia: The Westminster Press, 1989), 63ff.

[28]Cohen, Shaye J. D., Ed., *From the Maccabees to the Mishnah* (1987. Philadelphia: The Westminster Press, 1989), 63ff.

[29]Schweizer, E., *Matthew*, 49.

that Elijah will precede the coming of the Messiah.

The baptism story provides scriptural support for baptism as an initiation rite in the early church, but there was no such rite; baptism was not an initiation rite in Judaism until the 5th century CE. It is true that in the *Testaments of the Twelve Patriarchs* there is a passage involving the "Spirit of understanding and sanctification" resting upon Jesus "in the water," but the editors of HCNT point out that "in the water" is an apparent Christian interpolation.[30] In the Dead Sea Scrolls water ablutions are referred to, but they are not one time initiation rites; they are repeatable purification rituals. In addition, in Judaism baptism was never associated with forgiveness of sins at any time.[31]

Baptism of Jesus

When Jesus comes up out of the water, the physical heavens are "torn apart" and the Spirit descends on him like a dove (Mk 1.10). At Mt 3.16 the dove visibly alights on Jesus, and at Lk 3.22 the dove appears "in bodily form." Yet the crowds make no response to this visible phenomenon, indicating that the dove was a late addition to the scene.

Mark again finds the *Jewish Scriptures* useful in creating his Jesus. In Ezekiel the heavens open and the prophet sees "visions of God" (Ez 1.1). Isaiah writes that the spirit of the Lord was upon him because God had anointed him (61.1). God takes some of the spirit off Moses and places it on the 70 elders (Num 11.25). Elijah parts the Jordan River, crosses, and is taken up to heaven and Elisha, his disciple, receives a double portion of his master's spirit (2 Kgs 2.9,15). S. Lachs writes, "In Jewish sources, the dove is the symbol of the Holy Spirit or ...is used metaphorically as the Holy Spirit."[32] However, for Mark the Holy Spirit is not merely a symbol, but takes a physical form.

As we will see in the chapters that follow, often when a Jewish idea parallels a pagan one it is retained, but when Jewish and pagan ideas are in conflict the pagan idea is preferred. A spirit sent to serve a person was an idea more common among

---

[30]Boring, M., HCNT, 50-51, #21.

[31]Lachs, S., *Commentary*, 37.

[32]Lachs, S., *Commentary*, 46.

pagans than among Jews. In a Magical Greek Papyri,[33] a pagan magician says that the recipient must perform a rite so that the Lord of the Air will send him a spirit who will serve him, obeying all his commands:

> The recipient is to pray. A sign will occur: A hawk "will deliver you a... stone and then return to heaven ...you will perceive the angel whom you besought, sent to you, and you will promptly learn the counsels of the gods ...he will respond concisely to whatever you wish."[34]

Three of the parallels listed by M. Smith between this rite and the baptism of Jesus are:[35]

- A bird descends on the initiate. In pagan lore a bird was often seen as a messenger of God. The manifestation of a spirit as a bird appears in another magical papyrus where the initiate achieves a nature "equal to God."[36]

- The spirit enables the initiate to do miracles. In Mark, Matthew and Luke, Jesus displays miraculous powers only after the Spirit descends on him at his baptism.

- The initiate will be worshiped as a god. Jesus is worshiped by the wise men in the birth story of Matthew, and in Luke by the shepherds (Mt 2.11; Lk 2.20), by the women who came to the empty tomb, and by believers after his resurrection.

God's Son

After the spirit descends on Jesus, a voice from heaven says to Jesus, "You are my Son, the Beloved; with you I am well pleased" (Mk 1.11; cf. Ps 2.7; Isa 42.1). God is revealing to Jesus that he has been adopted by God as his son.

---

[33]Smith, Morton, *Jesus the Magician* 1978 (San Francisco: Harper, 1981), 98-100, PGM I.54ff Papyri graecae magicae, 2 ed., edd. K. Preisendanz and A. Henrichs, Stuttgart, 1973-1974, 2 vols.

[34]Smith, M., *Magician*, 129-130.

[35]Smith, M., *Magician*, 132.

[36]Smith, M., *Magician*, 14.

In Matthew (and Luke) the voice from heaven says to John and the crowds (Mt 3.17), "This is my son." Jesus already knew that he was the Son of God prior to his baptism. Matthew and Luke push Jesus' divinity back to his conception; in John's gospel Jesus is said to be eternally divine (Jn 1.1-3). The idea, "Son of God" or "God's son," appears in Ps 2.7 where the Lord speaking metaphorically to David, says, "You are my son...." and "You shall be a son to me" (1 Chr 17.13).[37] Other parallels include: Ex 4.22, "Israel is my first born son" and Dt 14.1 which refers to the Israelites as children of God. E. Schweizer grants that the details of the baptism of Jesus by John are "open to question."[38]

In various passages in the *Christian Scriptures*, the word *the* appears before the titles "Son of God," "Son of the Most High," "Son of the Blessed," and "Son of Man" indicating that there is a unique relationship between God and Jesus. Judaism allows no such exclusiveness between any person and the deity. In the Roman world, the titles "Son of God" and "Savior of the World" were applied to emperors, philosophers, divine men, and even athletes.

Excursus: The Embarrassment Theory

The "embarrassment theory" is often employed by modern apologists to defend the historicity of Jesus' baptism as well as other stories in the *Christian Scriptures*.[39] The theory holds, for example, that the church would not have created and preserved the baptism story which was so embarrassing to it unless it was in fact true. Therefore, it must be an actual historical event.

But the church which created the earliest layer of Mark, did not find the baptism account embarrassing. Jesus was depicted as an ordinary sinner whose sins are forgiven through the baptism by the Jewish prophet. Gerd Ludemann points out that "Jesus did not understand himself to be sinless."[40] Only at a

---

[37]Wansbrough, Henry, General Editor, *New Jerusalem Bible, The* (New York: Doubleday. 1990), 1615, n d.

[38]Schweizer, Eduard, *The Good News According to Mark* (Atlanta: John Knox Press, 1970), 37.

[39]Schweizer, E., *Mark*, 37.

[40]Ludemann, Gerd, *The Great Deception: And What Jesus Really Said and*

later time as Jesus' status increased did the story become embarrassing. Jesus is now divine, so the sandals, the idea that Jesus would baptize with the Holy Spirit, the voice from Heaven, etc., were added to Mark's original story.

Matthew further dilutes the embarrassment found in Mark by having the Baptist say that it is Jesus who should be baptizing him (Mt 4.14). At Lk 3.21, Luke has severed Jesus from the Baptist.[41] Jesus is far too divine in John's gospel, so John omits any mention of Jesus' baptism at all (cf. Jn 4.1-2). Jesus' superiority to the Baptist is even clearer in the later non-canonical *Gospel of the Nazoreans*. Jesus rejects the baptism of John saying, "Wherein have I sinned that I should go and be baptized by him?"[42]

All of this simply shows that the divine character of Jesus developed over time, not that the baptism actually occurred. One should not be surprised by the evolving portraits of Jesus or the Baptist. As we shall see, a number of characters in the gospels grow and develop over time.

The Temptation of Jesus

At Mark 1.12-13, the spirit drives Jesus into the wilderness where he stays with the wild beasts for forty days; he rejects Satan's (undescribed) temptations and is waited on by angels, all of which demonstrates the superior power of Jesus.

In the *Jewish Scriptures* people can be driven by the powerful Spirit of God.[43] The spirit of the Lord can pick Elijah up and throw him down on some safe mountain or in a valley (2 Kings 2.16). In Mark, the Spirit drives Jesus into the wilderness, but in Matthew and Luke the divine Jesus is led by the Spirit, not driven.

Matthew and Luke add that Jesus fasts in the wilderness for forty days (Mt 4.2, Lk 4.2) as Moses does for 40 days and 40 nights (Ex 34.28; cf Elijah 1 Kgs 19.8)[44]. In addition, it rains for forty days and nights during Noah's flood; David and Solomon

---

Did (Prometheus Books. 1999), 101.

[41] Beck, N., *Mature Christianity*, 200.

[42] Ibid., 101.

[43] Schweizer, E., *Mark*, 42; Cf. M. Smith, *Magician*, 211.

[44] Lachs, S. *Commentary*. 50

each rule forty years; Moses and his people wander for forty years in the wilderness, etc.[45]

In Matthew and Luke the divine Jesus says to the devil who is tempting him, you should not "put the Lord your God to the test...." (Mt 4.7; Lk 4.12; cf. Dt 6.16). Being tempted by a demonic ruler of the world is unknown in the *Jewish Scriptures*.[46] Satan in the Book of Job is wholly subordinate to the Lord and plays only a minor role in Judaism as compared to his later role in Christianity. Paul's letters, written only 10 to 20 years before Mark, know nothing of any temptation of Jesus by Satan.

The Galilean Ministry

Mark wrongly assumes throughout his gospel that Jews live only in certain cities and areas segregated from pagans. Galilee in northern Palestine and Judea in southern Palestine are depicted as Jewish. Pagan territory east of the Jordan River (the Decapolis or Ten Cities), Tyre, and Sidon are depicted as pagan cities or regions. This demographic scheme is artificial. The Mishnah (ca 200 CE) refers to cities and towns in Palestine which include both Jews and pagans.[47] Mark believes that Jews hated non-Jews and so lived apart from them.

Mark does not tell us how long the Galilean ministry of Jesus lasted; it could have been a few weeks or months, but no longer than a year since the Synoptics (the gospels of Mark, Matthew and Luke) mention only one Passover, an annual celebration. The idea of a three-year ministry comes from the gospel of John (written ca 100 CE) which the ancient Christian apologists use to interpret the earlier gospels!

After John the Baptist is arrested (Greek *delivered up*), Jesus begins to preach in Galilee, "the kingdom of God has come near; repent, and believe in the good news [gospel]" (Mk 1.14). Ancient mainstream Jews in the first century CE rarely spoke of the kingdom of God. Philo (d 50 CE) and Josephus (d 100 CE) held that the kingdom is present on earth and is not some future cosmic

[45]Funk Robert W., Ed., *The Acts of Jesus: The Search for the Authentic Deeds of Jesus* (Polebridge Press. 1998), 55

[46]Smith, M., *Magician*, 211.

[47]Neusner, Jacob, *The Mishnah: A New Translation* (New Haven and London: Yale University Press, 1988), Abodah Zarah, 4.11C.

event to be ushered in by "the Messiah." As E. Schweizer points out, the words *gospel* (good news), *preaching* and *repentance* (Mk 1.15) are "the language of the church (Acts 5:31; 11:18; 20:21),"[48] not Jesus. In what follows, we will find more early church beliefs and practices attributed to Jesus, making their acceptance easier.

Matthew states that Jesus leaves Nazareth and makes his home in Capernaum, "in the territory of Zebulon and Naphtali, so that what has been spoken through the prophet Isaiah might be fulfilled..." (Mt 4.12-14; Isa 9.1f). Matthew quotes Isaiah who describes Galilee as the land of "the Gentiles" (Mt 4.15; cf. Isa 9.1). There a pagan people were in "darkness [and] have seen a great light" (Isa 9.1) which, according to Matthew, refers to the gospel of Jesus (Mt 4.15-16). Jesus has come to save pagans, at least those who convert to Christianity, not Jews.

Jesus Calls His First Disciples: Mark 1.16-20

Walking by the Sea of Galilee, Jesus sees four fishermen at work and calls them as his first disciples. Simon (Peter) and his brother Andrew know nothing of any miracles or teachings of Jesus and yet instantly follow Jesus when he says, "Follow me and I will make you fish for people"(Mk 1.17). Philosophers, too, "fish for men."[49]

The magical call rarely appears in the *Jewish Scriptures* but at 1 Kgs 19.19-21 the prophet Elijah throws his mantle over Elisha who kisses his parents goodbye and sacrifices his oxen, distributing the meat among the people. He then follows Elijah. Miracles and teachings play no role in the call stories of Mark, Matthew, or 1 Kgs 19.

At Lk 5.1-11, Jesus preaches to Simon Peter but this does not induce him to follow Jesus. Instead, Jesus produces a miraculous catch of fish, after which Simon Peter as well as James and John (the sons of Zebedee) immediately follow Jesus, leaving "everything" (Lk 5.11). Herodotus writes of a story told by Cyrus of Persia about a great catch of fish.[50] In the *Jewish Scriptures* miracles never cause any conversions.

---

[48]Schweizer, E., *Mark*, 44.

[49]Schweizer, E., *Mark*, 48.

[50]Boring, M., HCNT, 207, #294.

In John's gospel, Andrew and an unnamed man hear the Baptist identify Jesus as the "Lamb of God" (Jn 1.36) and they join Jesus on that day. Nathaniel recognizes Jesus as "the Son of God" and "the king of Israel" and he and Philip immediately follow Jesus (Jn 1.49).

Diogenes Laertius relates a story of a citizen of Athens who is seeking virtue. He becomes a pupil of Socrates as soon as the philosopher says, "Follow me and learn."[51] Similarly, Xenophon hears Socrates say, "follow me" and he does so immediately.[52] Aristotle writes that a "Corinthian farmer, after coming into contact with" Plato's dialogue, Gorgias, "forthwith gave up his farm and his vines, put his soul under Plato's guidance..."[53] J. Fitzmyer concedes that the miraculous call fits in a pagan world as well as a Jewish one.[54]

Exorcisms and Healings

Jesus goes to Capernaum in Galilee and teaches in the synagogue on the Sabbath (Mk 1.21-28). Mark says that Jesus' Jewish hearers are amazed, for he preaches with "authority, and not as the scribes" (1.22). Mark is depicting Jesus as superior to the Jewish religious leaders.

Jesus does not teach like a rabbi. S. Lachs says real Jewish scribes and Pharisees would "teach the Oral Law by citing the authorities from whom the speaker received the traditions being transmitted."[55] E. Schweizer agrees and points out that ". . . the rabbis never could have conceived of a call so radical as to make clear that being with Jesus is more important than all of God's commandments (Mk 10.21)."[56] Quite true. Never.

In the synagogue, when Jesus expels an unclean spirit from a man (Mk 1.23), it cries out "What have you to do with us, Jesus of Nazareth? Have you come to destroy us?" (Mk 1.24). Jesus

---

[51] Balch, David L., Everett Ferguson, Wayne A. Meeks, Eds., *Greeks, Romans, and Christians: Essays in Honor of Abraham J. Malherbe* (Minneapolis: Fortress Press. 1990), 27.

[52] Ibid.

[53] Boring, M., HCNT,54, #27, Aristotle, "On Philosophy".

[54] Fitzmyer, Joseph A., S.J. *The Gospel According to Luke.* 2 vols. (The Anchor Bible. New York: Doubleday, 1981), vol 1, 546.

[55] Lachs, S., *Commentary*, 60, ref verse 1.27-28.

[56] Schweizer, E., *Mark*, 49.

has come to defeat evil cosmic powers. A stele in Egypt (525-337 BCE) states, "You come in peace, great God, destroyer of the evil ones."[57] Lucian has Ion refer "to those who free possessed men from their terrors by exorcising the spirits..."[58]

Again, Mark depicts Jewish religious leaders as impotent. They are unable to cast out unclean spirits but Jesus casts them out in a Jewish place of worship, and on the Sabbath at that. In the gospels, virtually no Jewish persons have sufficient faith to perform miracles other than the disciples of Jesus. Mark concludes by saying that Jesus' fame spread "throughout the surrounding region of Galilee" (Mk 1.28). Originally Jesus was an obscure figure. Mark created the summary statements that he uses to stress the popularity of Jesus.

Exorcisms are rare in Jewish tradition. The *Jewish Scriptures* and the works of the first-century CE writers, Josephus and Philo, contain no accounts of exorcisms.

After Jesus casts out the unclean spirit, he and his four disciples immediately leave the synagogue and go to the house of Simon Peter and Andrew (Mk 1.29-31). Peter's mother-in-law has a fever. Taking her hand, Jesus lifts her up and cures her.

Is Jesus violating the Sabbath by working (lifting her up)? A Jewish Jesus would know that a fever which threatened life could be healed even if labor were required. The rabbis in the Mishnah assert that even a minor eye problem could be treated, since it could lead to blindness, stumbling, and possibly death. But Mark does not say that the fever is life-threatening, so his Jesus appears to be violating Sabbath law.

Also, if Peter's mother-in-law was cooking or serving food on the Sabbath, she would be breaking the Sabbath law, as would Jesus and his disciples by accepting this service. Real Jews would have served themselves food which had been prepared before the Sabbath.

The Greek word used here for serves indicates a continuous, ongoing activity. Mark provides scriptural support for the subordinate role assigned to women in the early church. The high office of apostleship was not bestowed on women (the position of deaconess was an office of low status in the church). Christians

---

[57]Boring, M., HCNT, 172, #231.
[58]Boring, M., HCNT, 171-172, #230.

and pagans had no problem with allocating women a religious role as long as they were subordinate to male authority. Jesus was not a feminist.

In a summary statement, Mark writes that at sundown "the whole city" brought their sick and possessed whom Jesus healed, forbidding them to tell anyone who had helped them (part of the messianic secret by which Jesus conceals his identity and his mission). Mark says Jesus cures many people and casts out many demons (Mk 1.32-34); Matthew and Luke upgrade the status of Jesus: "all" are cured or exorcised (Mt 8.16-17; Lk 4.40).

At Mk 1.34, Jesus "does not permit demons to speak, because they knew him"(another part of the messianic secret). Originally, the demons were probably depicted as not having recognized Jesus. Paul, writing before Mark, says that none of the "rulers of this age" (spirits or *archons*) would have crucified Jesus if they had known who he was (1 Cor 2.7-8). Mark's depiction of Jesus' popularity with Jews is not believable since Jesus appears to violate Jewish law.

The Marcan Jesus tells his disciples that he and they should go to the neighboring towns throughout Galilee and "proclaim the message... for this is what I came out to do" (Mk 1.38). The disciples call him *rabbi* (teacher), and in Mark the Greek words for *taught* and *teaching* appear a total of twenty times,[59] but Jesus has not taught much up to this point. The gospels of Matthew and Luke are each about double the size of Mark, and almost all of the additional material consists of teachings attributed to Jesus. This raises his status from exorcist and wonder worker in Mark to that of teacher in Matthew and Luke.

Mark says that Jesus teaches in *their* synagogues (1.39). *Their*, not *our* synagogues? Is Jesus not Jewish?

In the *Jewish Scriptures*, cures by prophets are relatively rare and mostly confined to Moses, Elijah and Elisha.[60] God performs these miracles, or they are done at his will, but Jesus acts on his own authority. M. Smith notes that Jesus is depicted as superior to the prophets and religious leaders. For example, "Miriam's leprosy was healed by Moses' prayer and a leper in

---

[59]Schweizer, E., *Mark*, 50.
[60]Smith, M., *Magician*, 211.

Galilee [is cured] by Jesus' command" (Num. 12.13, Mk. 1.41).[61]
Also, "Jesus [tells] ten lepers to go to the priests" and they are
cured before they reach the Jewish priests (Lk 17.12ff).[62]

Mk 1.40-45 relates the story of a leper who kneels before Jesus and begs to be made clean. Jesus, like the Lord of the *Jewish
Scriptures*, is moved by pity. He cures the leper and then forbids
him to tell anyone. Jesus sends him away, telling him to present
himself to the priest (at the temple in Jerusalem, 80 miles away?)
and to do what Moses (not God?) has commanded as an offering
for his cleansing. E.P. Sanders considers this clear evidence of
Jesus' respect for the law (Lev. 14.2-9).[63] But we think it is by
no means clear that this is so. When the Jewish priest confirms
that the leper is clean, he would be testifying to the power of Jesus. The former leper goes out and tells so many people, "that
Jesus could no longer go into a town openly but stayed out in
the country" (Mk 1.45).

If a man had a lethal and contagious disease like leprosy, he
would not be allowed to appear in public places or to live in a
city or town.[64] This practice of keeping lepers apart from the
public is both a Jewish and a pagan practice, one intended to
check the spread of contagion. Herodotus (484 BCE) writes that
a leper may not enter a town and the great Greek historian, like
Jesus, thinks that the disease is caused by sin.[65]

Some apologists argue that Mark is referring to a noncconta-
gious minor skin ailment. The Greek word may be so translated,
but why would a man kneel before Jesus desperately begging for
the cure of a minor skin rash? Besides, the Synoptics indicate
that leprosy is meant. This story of the leper is unhistorical;
no location is given, and no disciples or witnesses are present.
Matthew finally provides a setting by placing it at the foot of the
mountain after Jesus' Sermon on the Mount (Mt 8.1ff).

---

[61]Smith, M., *Magician*, 212.

[62]Smith, M., *Magician*, 212.

[63]Sanders, E.P., *Historical Figure*, 129.

[64]Cotter, Wendy, *Miracles in Greco-Roman Antiquity: A Sourcebook* (Routledge. 1999), 221-228.

[65]Boring, M., HCNT, 64, #49.

Chapter 2

Condemning Jewish Law

And when his family heard it, they went out to seize him, for people were saying, "He is beside himself."
— Mark 3.21

No longer will anyone say that I am crazy, I who am a [pagan] prophetess of the great God.
— Sibylline Oracles 3.811-18, 3rd Century BCE

Mark 2.1-3.6 is made up of five consecutive stories involving hostility between Jesus and Jewish religious leaders.

Forgiving Sins

In the first conflict story (Mk 2.1-12), a crowd seeking to be healed by Jesus is so large that it blocks the entrance to "his home" in Capernaum of Galilee (Mk 2.1). Four people climb to the roof and dig through the ceiling, lowering a paralyzed man on a mat into the house. Jesus is moved by the faith of those who brought the man to him.

Jesus says to the paralytic, "your sins are forgiven," and some scribes think Jesus is guilty of blasphemy, since only God can forgive sins (Mk 2.5-7). Jesus, reading their minds, cures the man so that the scribes will know "the Son of Man has authority on earth to forgive sins" (Mk 2.10). The man exits the house. Through the crowd blocking the door? The Jewish Messiah has co-opted the divine prerogative of forgiving sins. We agree with E. Schweizer who concludes that the forgiveness material was

31

added to an original story about a healing[1] (cf. Ps 32.5; Isa 43.25).

Dinner With Tax Collectors and Sinners

In the second conflict story (Mk 2.13-17), Jesus dines at the house of his disciple, Levi, with "many tax collectors and sinners" (Mk 2.15). The scribes of the Pharisees object to this and Jesus counters, "Those who are well have no need of a physician, but those who are sick" (Mk 2.17).

Medical metaphors were very common in the ancient world. Diogenes Laertius reports that Antithsenes was criticized "for keeping company with evil men..." and the philosopher responds by saying that a physician treats a patient without getting the fever himself.[2] Jesus adds that he has come to save not the righteous, but sinners (Mk 2.17). Lucian (120-185 CE) writes, "Demonax... though he assailed sins, he forgave sinners, thinking that one should pattern after doctors, who heal sickness but feel no anger at the sick."[3]

N. Beck[4] writes that, "The presence of the scribes of the Pharisees as observers of the meal" is one of the reasons why some scholars think this story is fiction. How do Jesus' enemies know that he and his disciples were dining with sinners and tax farmers? Are the enemies of Jesus dining with him? Or are they looking through the windows? As to their function in the story, they are there to criticize Jesus.

This dining story is very popular with many contemporary Christian exegetes. M. Borg, for example, argues that Jesus was a champion of outcasts, a kind of hippie who broke the social boundaries which separate Jews and non-Jews, the rich and the poor, males and females, slaves and free, etc. But none of these outcasts are depicted as present at the dinner. Nor does Jesus elsewhere in Mark socialize with prostitutes, women, slaves, pagans, the poor, or the sick except for a former (?) leper at Mk 14.3. We don't know who the sinners are at dinner. In "Table Talk," Plutarch relates that "the rich should dine with the

---

[1]Schweizer, E., *Mark*, 62.
[2]Boring, M., HCNT, 75, #70.
[3]Boring, M., HCNT, 74, #66, Demonax 7.
[4]Beck, N., *Mature Christianity*, 144.

poor,"[5] a practice common with Stoics and members of the mystery cults.

Fasting

In the third conflict tale (Mk 2.18-22), the disciples of John the Baptist and those of the Pharisees ask Jesus why his disciples do not fast. Real Jews would fast at least on the most important Jewish holy day, the Day of Atonement, as well as at "times of special need."[6] Jesus replies that wedding guests do not fast until the "bridegroom is taken away from them" (Mk 2.20). This is the first and only time that Jesus hints at his death before he predicts it at Mk 8.31. Many scholars believe that Jesus was not originally associated with the bridegroom; neither the disciples nor anyone else responds to this allusion to his death. Nor is there a response to the saying about putting a new patch on an old cloak which implies that Judaism will be discarded (Mk 2.21-23)

This pericope has no location. It is a product of the church which needed to show that Jesus was aware of his upcoming death, and that Judaism was to be superseded by Christianity. Mark also has provided scriptural support for those Christians who believed in fasting (Mk 2.20; Mt 9.15; Lk 5.35). The Didache of the second century (8.1) names Wednesday and Friday as days of fasting for Christians.[7]

Incidentally, N. Beck is amused that Luke or his editor has added a verse in his parallel, "No one after drinking old wine desires new wine..." (Lk 5.39) thus unwittingly endorsing "the older wine — Jewish religion and culture!"[8]

Plucking Grain

In the fourth conflict story (Mk 2.23-28), the earliest evangelist writes that Jesus and his disciples are "making their way" through the grain fields on a Sabbath. His disciples pluck some

---

[5]Ibid., 428, "Table Talk", I,2.3.
[6]Schweizer, E., *Mark*, 68.
[7]Schweizer, E., *Mark*, 68.
[8]Beck, N., *Mature Christianity*, 203.

heads of grain to eat. "The Pharisees" pop up and criticize Jesus for allowing his disciples to do "what is not lawful on the Sabbath" (Mk 2.24), i.e., working. E. Schweizer says, "this story appears to be fictitious."[9]

In his defense, Jesus argues that David went to the house of God where the high priest Abiathar gave him bread which was reserved exclusively for priests (1 Sam 21.1-6). If the high priest can set aside the law, why can't Jesus do the same?

How good is Jesus' argument? First, the circumstances of David and Jesus are not analogous. David was not seeking food on the Sabbath, and the future king was acting in a wartime emergency. Jesus' disciples may have been hungry (as Matthew finally says at 12.1) but no emergency is implied. Second, Abiathar was the son of the high priest, Ahimelech, the man who actually helped David (1 Sam 21.1). Matthew and Luke drop the reference to the high priest.

Matthew adds an additional argument. The *Jewish Scriptures* allow the temple priests to *desecrate* (NRSV *break*) the Sabbath law by performing sacrifices, and yet the priests are "guiltless" (Mt 12.5). The *Jewish Scriptures* allow sacrifice, circumcision, and certain other rites to be performed on the Sabbath in the temple, for laws can be set aside. For example, if necessary to save a life one is required to labor on the Sabbath. However, a Jewish teacher would certainly know that performing a religious ritual is not *desecrating* the Sabbath.

At the end of the grain field story, Jesus preaches that, "The Sabbath was made for humankind, and not humankind for the Sabbath" (Mk 2.27). The rabbis agreed that, "The Sabbath is given over to you, not you to the Sabbath."[10] But the saying, "the Son of Man is lord even of the Sabbath" (Mk 2.28), is anti-Jewish and non-Jewish because Jesus (the Son of Man) makes himself equal to God. Matthew and Luke omit the Jewish saying about the Sabbath being given to humans, but keep the anti-Jewish saying that Jesus is lord of the Sabbath.

Plutarch relates that the Spartans said, "Because the laws ought to have authority over men, and not men over the laws..."

---

[9]Schweizer, E., *Mark*, 70.
[10]Boring, M., HCNT, 173, #233, Mekilta on Ex 31.13, 3rd century CE.

ancient laws should not be changed.[11] M. Smith points out that abolishing ancient customs was punishable by death under Roman law.[12] This is one reason why Jesus and Paul have difficulty justifying their nullification of ancient Jewish law and custom.

Healing of a Man with a Withered Hand

In the fifth and final conflict story in the cycle (Mk 3.1-6), Jesus cures a man with a withered hand in the synagogue on a Sabbath. His enemies have been watching him so that "they might accuse him" of violating Sabbath law (Mk 3.1-2,6). Would Jesus' enemies have believed that he could perform miraculous healings?[13] Jesus reads their minds and seeing the trap, seeks to foil them by asking, "'Is it lawful to do good or to do harm on the Sabbath, to save life or to kill?' But they were silent" (Mk 3.4). Jesus then heals the man's hand. In pagan tradition, cures of disabilities involving hands, legs, eyes, ears, etc., were common. For example, according to Dio Cassius, the Emperor Vespasian cured a man with a withered hand.[14]

The scene is a good example of Jesus' non-dialogues. Jesus' enemies fall into silence, unable to refute his superior teachings. How would Jewish religious leaders have answered him if they were not straw men? They would have known that doing good on the Sabbath is a fundamental Jewish value, and that saving a life is obligatory on any day, Sabbath or not. It has been so in Jewish tradition for thousands of years. In Mark and Matthew, the choice is not between life and death, since the man with the withered hand is in no danger of dying. The choice is whether to wait until sunset when the Sabbath ends, or not to wait. The "Jewish Messiah" chooses not to wait.

Here again Jesus shows no special concern for the sick or disabled person being healed.[15] Beck is right when he writes, "The fundamental purpose of Mk 3.1-6 is to depict the dumbness, the silence, and the callousness of those who oppose the developing

---

[11]Boring, M., HCNT, 174, #234.

[12]Boring, M., HCNT, #234.

[13]Schweizer, E., *Mark*, 74.

[14]Martin, F., 165.

[15]Beck, N., *Mature Christianity*, 147.

traditions of the followers of Jesus."[16] At Mk 3.6 Jesus' enemies are at last identified as Pharisees.[17] They leave the synagogue and conspire with the Herodians to figure out "how to destroy him" (Mk 3.6; Mt 12.14; cf. Lk 6.11). Why? What serious crime has he committed?

In Hebrew, there is no word which precisely corresponds to the Christian idea of *sin*. In Judaism, a sin is "An action which breaks a law or alternatively, the failure to observe a positive COMMANDMENT."[18] This would include any action or thought which violates the commandments of God, whether written or unwritten (oral, not in the *Jewish Scriptures*). "[T]he sinner is morally accountable to God, both for sins against man and for infractions of the ritual law."[19]

Wigoder, co-editor of the *Encyclopedia of Judaism*, points out that there are nearly 30 different words in the Tanakh which are associated with various kinds of sins. The most important is *het* (Hebrew) which occurs almost 600 times in the *Jewish Scriptures*; the root meaning is "to miss the mark... [I]t is the only term which describes the *least* offensive category of sin: an unwitting transgression of the ritual law."[20] (Wigoder's ital.).

The third most common term is *pesha*. It is usually translated as *transgress*, and refers to an offense more serious than *het* or *avon*. *Pesha* is the term for the most serious sin, and "is never used to refer explicitly to a ritual sin."[21] In other words, even if Jesus had inadvertently violated the Sabbath law (het), this would not have been a serious offense. E.P. Sanders[22] writes that even if Jesus had committed a minor violation of Sabbath law and then presented his legal defense, all a Jewish magistrate would say is, take "two doves as a sin offering when you are next in Jerusalem."

It is E.P. Sanders' opinion that the real Jesus was law obser-

---

[16]Ibid.

[17]Ibid.

[18]This information comes primarily from G. Wigoder's *Encyclopedia of Judaism*.

[19]*Encyclopedia of Judaism*, 658.

[20]*Encyclopedia of Judaism*, 659.

[21]*Encyclopedia of Judaism*, 659.

[22]Sanders, E.P., *Jewish Law from Jesus to the Mishnah* (Philadelphia: Trinity Press International, 1990), 90; The Mishnah, Shabbat 7.1.

vant throughout his life except for minor violations.[23] Against him, E. Schweizer writes, "Undoubtedly, Jesus' frequent transgressing of the Sabbath commandment in his preaching and in his conduct is historical."[24] Maybe E. Schweizer is right, but why would a Jewish teacher discard the commandments of God? And if he had engaged in serious violations of law, why was he not so charged at his Jewish trial in Jerusalem? And why would a non-Jewish Jesus attract so many Jewish followers?

What motivation does Jesus attribute to the homicidal Pharisees? Jesus is angry and grieves at "their hardness of heart" (Mk 3.5). Jesus grieves for his enemies, the Pharisees (see Mk 7). Matthew and Luke omit this. Neither Jesus nor Mark gives any motivation for the murderous enmity of the Herodians. Do the Herodians see Jesus as a political threat? Do they think that he is claiming to be a king? In Exodus the phrase "hardness of heart" is applied to, among others, the evil Pharaoh who tries to stop Moses from freeing the Hebrew people from slavery in Egypt. In the *Christian Scriptures*, virtually all Jews and Jewish religious leaders are depicted as "hardened of heart," i.e., unable or unwilling to perceive Jesus' truth.

Most scholars agree that Mark himself created the summary statements in his gospel. Mk 3.7-12 is typical. He writes, "a great multitude from Galilee" followed Jesus (Mk 3.7), many coming to him to be cured. They came "from Judea, Jerusalem, Idumea, beyond the Jordan, and the [pagan] region around Tyre and Sidon." Many are healed by touching Jesus. Jesus asks the disciples to prepare a boat so that when the crush of the crowd becomes too great, he can escape.

Mark relates that when "unclean spirits saw [Jesus], they fell down before him and shouted, 'You are the Son of God!'" (Mk 3.11). Jesus commanded the spirits "not to make him known" (Mk 3.12; cf. Mk 1.25) and apparently the evil spirits always obeyed, as none of the gospels report otherwise. Neither the disciples, the people who have been exorcised, nor witnesses show any reaction when Jesus is called "the Son of God" at Mk 3.11, or when he exorcises people, or silences the demons. Many Greek heroes were noted for healing diseases, including Hercules and

---

[23]Sanders, E.P., *Historical Jesus*, 252.

[24]Schweizer, E., *Mark*, 76.

Asclepius, the god of healing, but they probably did not attempt to keep their identity secret by silencing people or demons.

Jesus Appoints the Twelve

Jesus had ordered the disciples to prepare a boat (Mk 3.9), but at Mk 3.13 we find that Jesus is up on "the mountain." The boat has disappeared and will not reappear until Mk 4.1. This is one of many errors in Mark which show that his gospel has been much edited. Matthew and Luke omit the boat.

Jesus calls "those whom he wanted" and appoints twelve, designating them *apostles* (Mk 3.13-14). Some manuscripts of Mark omit the appointing of the twelve and others omit his list of the twelve.[25] Mark's list at 3.16-19 conflicts with the other three lists at Mt 10.2-4, Lk 6.14-15, and Acts 1.13. We will comment on only a single problem relating to the list, one that concerns Levi.

In Mark's list the name *Matthew* is listed, not Levi, although Levi was called as a disciple after the first four. The second gospel also has "Matthew" (Mt 9.9; cf. Mk 2.14). Levi never appears in his gospel nor does the name appear in the list of the twelve in Acts of the Apostles (1.13). Matthew or his editor has added "Matthew" to the twelve. Why? The twelve had high status in the early church, as we can see when Jesus says, "when the Son of Man is seated on the throne of his glory, you who have followed me will also sit on twelve thrones, judging the twelve tribes of Israel" (Mt 19.28; cf. Lk 22.30). Matthew's association with the twelve increased his status, which in turn made it easier for the early church to accept the gospel falsely ascribed to him.

Until the twelve are chosen at Mk 3.14, Jesus has referred to only five disciples. Some scholars think that Jesus may have had only three or four disciples. Burton L. Mack thinks that Jesus may have had none.[26] Mark drew on collections of teachings and acts attributed to Jesus that included no disciples. The title apostles is applied to the twelve only three times in Mark and Matthew and is probably a late addition (Mk 3.14, 6.30 and Mt

---

[25]NRSV, 52, fn. z, a.

[26]Mack, Burton L., *A Myth of Innocence; Mark and Christian Origins* (Philadelphia: Fortress Press, 1988, 1st paperback 1991), 79 fn. 1.

10.2).[27] Luke uses the title five times, and John never applies *apostle* or *apostles* to the twelve.

E. Schweizer writes, "There is some doubt whether Jesus chose a more limited circle of twelve disciples."[28] The twelve are only loosely connected to the gospel stories, "usually appear[ing] in editorial statements."[29] Schweizer adds that in Jewish tradition a group of twelve leaders is virtually unknown. In 1 Corinthians and Acts some missionaries are called *apostles*, but the term is applied only to those not associated with the twelve.

Jesus' True Family: Mark 3.19b-35

Mark says that Jesus is a teacher, yet the only teaching of Jesus presented so far is his preaching about the nearness of the kingdom of God (Mk 1.14).

The story about Jesus' family and Beelzebul is one of eight "sandwich" stories in Mark's gospel. (A sandwich story occurs when one story is begun, interrupted by another, and then resumed.) Mark interrupts the true family story with an incident about Beelzebul and then continues the first story.

Jesus and his disciples enter his home. A crowd comes, pressing so heavily that Jesus and his disciples are not able to eat (Mk 3.19b-20). People have been saying that Jesus is crazy. Jesus' mother and brothers hear this and, believing he is crazy, attempt to reach him in order to restrain him (Mk 3.21).

Pagans knew about wisdom and madness, too. Alciphorn writes that a father, whose son had converted to Cynicism, said he was possessed by an evil spirit which drove him out of his mind.[30] In the Sibylline Oracles 3.811-18 (3rd cent. BCE), a prophetess discloses the wisdom of god; "no longer will anyone say that I am crazy, I who am a prophetess of the great God."[31]

Inserted into the family story is the incident at Mk 3.22-29. Here, the scribes from Jerusalem pop up and accuse Jesus of being able to cast out demons because he is possessed by Beelze-

---

[27] Schweizer, E., *Mark*, 129.

[28] Schweizer, E., *Mark*, 127.

[29] Schweizer, E., *Mark*, 127, 128.

[30] Boring, M., HCNT, 174, #235, Letters of Farmers, "Euthydicus to Philiscus" 38.

[31] Boring, M., HCNT, 175, #236.

bul, the ruler of the demons. Jesus counters with, "How can Satan cast out Satan?"

After the Beelzebul insertion, Mark resumes his story about the family. Jesus' mother and his brothers have come to the house but are unable to enter due to the crowd. They send Jesus a message asking him to come out to them (Mk 3.31). Jesus responds with a shocking teaching. He rejects his family, saying, "Here are my mother and my brothers! Whoever does the will of God is my brother and sister and mother" (Mk 3.34-35).

The pagan philosophers also wrote about choosing loyalty to wisdom over loyalty to one's family. In a letter of the second century CE, a pagan father states that, "a fit of anger" which came from an evil spirit came on his son and "drove him out of his mind." He had become a Cynic and now ignores his parents.[32] The real family of the Cynic philosophers were those who accepted Cynic teachings.[33] Epictetus, the Stoic, writes, "Man, the Cynic has made all mankind his children; the men among them he has as sons, the women as daughters; in that spirit he approaches them all and cares for them all."[34] Musonius Rufus writes in Must One Obey One's Parents Under All Circumstances? (30-100 CE), "Your father forbids you to study philosophy, but the common father of all men and gods, Zeus, bids you and exhorts you to do so."[35] He also says that if your father forbids you to study philosophy, you may disobey him.[36]

E. Schweizer writes, "There is scarcely any other passage where Mark's pen is as evident as it is"[37] in the true family story.

Jesus' relatives do not merely reject his religious mission, but in the original story they believe he is a slave of Beelzebul or Satan. The story was changed in order to rehabilitate Jesus' mother and his siblings. Jesus' status had grown within the early church and with it that of his family. The church no longer wanted to see the family portrayed so negatively. For example, James, the brother of Jesus, is the head of the Jerusalem church (Acts 15.13-19; Gal 2.9,12) and Mary is shown as a be-

---

[32]Boring, M., HCNT, 174, #325.

[33]Boring, M., HCNT, 222, #327.

[34]Boring, M., HCNT, 119, #148, Epictetus Discourses 3.22.81-82.

[35]Boring, M., HCNT, 192, #264; see also Musonius Rufus HCNT, 221 #325.

[36]Boring, M., HCNT, 192, #264.

[37]Schweizer, E., *Mark*, 83.

liever in Acts 1.14 and in John where she appears at the foot of the cross (Jn 19.25-27). Thus, the accusation that Jesus was allied with Beelzebul or Satan is shifted away from the family; now the scribes from Jerusalem claim that Jesus is possessed. Luke wants not a whisper about the family's faithlessness. The "true family" material is separated from the Beelzebul story (Lk 8.19-21; Lk 11.14-16). In the gospels of Matthew and Luke there is no reference to the family believing that Jesus is crazy, much less that he is possessed.

But in Mark why does Jesus denigrate his own family? Pagans converted to Christianity and some undoubtedly alienated their families by rejecting the parents' pagan religious beliefs. Jesus explicitly encourages people to choose Jesus over their own families; he preaches that those who have left "house or brothers or sisters or mother or father or children or fields, for my sake and for the sake of the good news" will be rewarded a hundredfold in family and property and will receive eternal life in the age to come (Mk 10.29-30). But family was sacred in the Greco-Roman world and so the editors of Mark and Matthew softened this attack on the family. Jesus quotes Moses saying that one should honor one's parents, and "Whoever speaks evil of father or mother must surely die..." {Mk 7.10; Mt 15.5). Also, in the story of the rich young man, Jesus requires people to "Honor [their] father and mother" in order to inherit eternal life (Mk 10.19).

The "true family" story is another example of Jesus' non-dialogues with his "opponents" (Mk 3.22-30). The scribes from Jerusalem accuse Jesus of working miracles through Beelzebul. When Jesus argues, "How can Satan cast out Satan?" (Mk 3.22-23), his enemies can think of no response and disappear from the story. Pseudo debates like this appear throughout the four gospels. They usually consist of a hostile objection to Jesus' teachings or the behavior of Jesus or his disciples. Jesus then harangues his opponents with a tongue-lashing monologue to which there is no response other than silence. The Pharisees, scribes, chief priests, etc., are simply foils for Jesus' diatribes (see Mk 7.1-23; Mt 23.1-36; Lk 11.39-52).

Sin Against the Holy Spirit: Mk 3.28-29

Near the end of Mark Chapter 3, Jesus teaches that all sins and
blasphemies can be forgiven except blasphemy against the Holy
Spirit (Mk. 3.28-29). In Matthew and Luke Jesus preaches that
blasphemy even against the Son of Man (Jesus) is forgivable (Mt
12.31-32; Lk 12.10). Many Christians are shocked and puzzled
by this teaching. They needn't be. This saying was added by the
church because after Jesus was gone, it claimed that its spiritual
guidance came solely from the Holy Spirit. How else could the
church justify new rules, beliefs and practices? To blaspheme
the Holy Spirit was to reject the authority of the church. John
realizes that after Jesus' death, he will no longer be present to
supply truth, so his Jesus states that the Father will send the
Holy Spirit (the *paraclete*) to teach the disciples and remind them
of what Jesus has taught (Jn 14.26).

Chapter 3

Blinding the Jews

For those outside [the kingdom of God], everything comes in parables; in order that they may indeed look, but not perceive, and indeed listen, but not understand... so that they may not turn again and be forgiven.
— Mark 4.11-12

Communicate this to no one else, but hide it, by Helios, since you have been thought worthy by the Lord God to receive this great mystery.
— Magical Papyrus of Paris IV.475-830

Agricultural Parables: Mk 4.1-34

The Sower: Mk 4.1-20; 21-25

Jesus, sitting with his disciples in a boat on "the sea," speaks in parables to "a very large crowd" on the shore (Mk 4.1). He tells how the seed is sown by the sower, falling on the path, rocky ground, and among thorns, but none of the seed produces grain. Some seed falls on good soil and, without birds or thorns to hinder it, produces bountiful crops, thirty- and sixty- and a hundred-fold.

Later, Jesus is alone with "those who were around him" and the twelve (Mk 4.10). (Note the vague reference to those other than the twelve. The editor of Mark is harmonizing the gospel with Luke which depicts Jesus as having many disciples and followers.) They ask Jesus about the parables, (though he explains only one) and he tells them in plain language that Satan, worldly concerns, and persecutions cause some to fall away from the

43

word (leave the religion), but the seeds on good soil grow and bear fruit, i.e., produce a lasting religious commitment.

What is the meaning of the sower? It deals with a universal problem, one found in all religions. If one's faith is true, why is it that some abandon their faith while others do not?

Most serious scholars ascribe the sower parable and Jesus' explanation of it to the early church. Many words appear in the parables which are found only in the letters of the early church.[1]

Jesus says all that is hidden will be revealed; in the future the church will teach all in plain language (4.21-22), that is, after his death. He teaches that the kingdom of God is like a seed which grows in a secret and mysterious way which the believer need not understand or even be aware of; the sower can then sleep night after night while the plants mature. Matthew, Luke, and John interpreted the Marcan Jesus as teaching that the spread of the faith requires no human effort. In other words, God alone causes the church to grow. This saying was threatening to the missionary work of the early church, so the later gospel writers omit it.

Burton L. Mack in his influential book, *A Myth of Innocence*, points out that the sower and other seed parables were common in the world of pagan rhetoric.[2] He writes, "The 'sower' was a stock analogy for the 'teacher,' 'sowing' for 'teaching,' 'seed' for 'words,' and 'soils' for 'students'."[3] Even in the 21st century, we still talk about teachers "sowing the seeds of wisdom" in their students.

Mark's use of agricultural metaphors does not prove that Jesus operated in a rural setting. Pastoral writing by urban-ites, including images of shepherds and sheep and sowing seed, etc., were well known in Greek and Roman literature long before Mark. Aristotle writes of a farmer who, after reading Plato's di-alogue, Gorgias, "forthwith gave up his farm and his vines, put his soul under Plato's guidance, and made it a seed-bed and a planting ground for Plato's philosophy."[4]

B. Mack emphasizes the use of agricultural metaphors by the

---

[1]Schweizer, E., *Mark*, 96.
[2]Mack, B., *Myth*, 160.
[3]Ibid.
[4]Boring, M., HCNT, 54, #27, Aristotle, "On Philosophy".

Cynic philosophers,[5] but there is no need to do so. Stoics influenced early Christianity more than the Cynics did and they were familiar with such figures of speech. The Roman Stoic, Seneca (d 65 CE) writes,[6] the "word should be scattered like seed; no matter how small the seed may be, if it once has found favorable ground, it unfolds its strength and from an insignificant thing spreads to its greatest growth."[7] Jesus teaches that the smallest seed is the mustard seed, and yet it grows and "becomes the greatest of all shrubs" (Mk 4.30). Though starting small, the faith or church will grow and blossom.

Divine Deception

The Purpose of Parables

Before Jesus relates the parables, the twelve "and others" had asked Jesus why he teaches the Jewish crowd only in parables. Jesus replies, "To you has been given the secret of the kingdom of God, but for those outside, everything comes in parables..." (Mk 4.11). Why? So the Jewish people (the crowds) will not understand and be saved. In view of the Holocaust, many modern Christians are shocked by this anti-Jewish teaching and many apologists have tried to interpret it away, but Jesus' meaning is quite clear. He says they are taught in parables, in "order that 'they may indeed look, but not perceive, and may indeed listen, but not understand; so that they may not turn again [to God] and be forgiven'" (Mk 4.12). Jesus is concealing the kingdom; Jews are predestined to hell!

The disciples are cautioned not to tell anyone. The "messianic secret" involves Jesus hiding his mission, as well as his identity. The secret is revealed through three activities of Jesus:

- He commands the unclean spirits not to reveal who he is, and orders the people whom he has cured or exorcised not to reveal who aided them. (Note that Jesus assumes the Messiah could be identified by his miracles, but in Jewish tradition the Messiah does not work miracles.)

---

[5]Mack, B., *Myth*, 160.

[6]Seneca, *Letters from a Stoic*, Selected and translated by Robin Campbell (London/New York: Penguin Books, 1969), Epistle 38:2.

[7]Mack, B., *Myth*, 159.

- He teaches the crowds only in parables so they will not understand and be saved.

- Jesus (or God) hardens their hearts (minds), so they are spiritually blind (sometimes "the Jews" themselves harden their own hearts).

Ancient pagans, too, believed in secrecy. "Myths have been used by inspired poets, by the best of philosophers, by those who established the mysteries, and by the gods themselves in oracles."[8] The Pythagoreans taught their disciples to keep secret the "divine mysteries and methods of instruction..."[9] After communicating a magical formula, a pagan magician says, "Share this great mystery with no one [else], but conceal it, by Helios, since you have been deemed worthy by the lord"[10] (cf. Mk 1.44).

Many pagans thought that the wise person interprets myths allegorically, i.e., symbolically, ignoring the literal sense. Sallustius writes that only "the ignorant Egyptians" and others would believe that earth is Isis, moisture is Osiris, water Kronos, and so on. He asserts that various myths are suitable for philosophers and poets. Some are suitable for ". . . religious initiations, since every initiation aims at uniting us with the world and the gods."[11] For Sallustius the revered myths and literature must be symbolically interpreted in order to reconcile them with sophisticated values and thought. Similarly, using symbolic interpretation writers of the *Christian Scriptures* sought to harmonize the *Jewish Scriptures* with Christian beliefs.

Sermon on the Mount: Mt 4.24-7.29; Lk 6.17-7.1

Mark's gospel contains very little of the teachings of Jesus found in Matthew's Sermon on the Mount and Luke's Sermon on the Plain, but we will briefly consider some of these ethical teachings as they are still assumed by many to be unique to Christianity.

---

[8]MacMullen, Ramsay and Eugene N. Lane, Eds., *Paganism and Christianity 100-425 CE: A Sourcebook* (Minneapolis: Fortress Press, 1992), 274, quoting Sallustius, On the Gods and Ordered Creation.

[9]Boring, M., HCNT, 92, #98.

[10]Boring, M., HCNT, 64, #50, PGM 1.130-32.

[11]MacMullen and Lane, 275.

In Matthew, Jesus goes up to "the mountain" to escape the crowds and, when his disciples join him, he delivers the Sermon on the Mount (Mt 5.1).

Matthew, like Mark, says that Jesus teaches the crowds only in parables, but after three chapters of teachings expressed in plain language, the gospel writer informs us that "the crowds were astounded at his teaching" (7.28-29). Lachs writes that, "the Sermon was apparently intended only for the disciples."[12]

Similarly, Luke says that Jesus chose the twelve and then came down from the mountain to a level place (Lk 6.17) where he delivers his Sermon on the Plain. Luke says that Jesus had "finished all his sayings in the hearing of the people" (Lk 7.1). Most scholars agree with Lachs that originally only the disciples heard the sermons, the crowds were added by the early church. Why? The church wanted to depict Jesus as one who was open to all — a popular view among today's Christians. It was necessary to rehabilitate the elitist and secretive Jesus of Mark.

Jesus teaches outdoors in a sitting position. This is anachronistic since in 30 CE it was customary to teach indoors and to stand while preaching (cf. Mt 5.1).[13] Most scholars agree with Lachs that the locale for the sermon is intended to parallel the receipt of the law by Moses on Mt. Sinai (Ex 19.1ff).[14] The purpose of the sermon is to depict Jesus as a teacher who supersedes Moses. For example, "Blessed are the poor in spirit" (Mt 5.3) is derived from Psalms of Solomon 10.7.[15] The "poor" in Jewish literature refers to the people of God, i.e., Jews, but for Matthew, it refers to the Christians.

At Mt 5.17-20, Jesus says that he has not come to abolish the law or the prophets, but to "fulfill" them; fulfill means "to complete." At Mt 5.18 Jesus says not one iota of the law is to be erased. We agree with Lachs that this "borders on sophistry..."[16] Jesus refers to basic Jewish moral laws which Jesus "improves on" but does not reject.

Mt 5.21-26 is the first of six passages which states a Jewish law and then compares it to a teaching of Jesus, to the detriment

---

[12]Lachs, S., *Commentary* 67.

[13]Lachs, S., *Commentary* 67-68.

[14]Lachs, S., *Commentary* 67.

[15]Lachs, S., *Commentary* 71.

[16]Lachs, S., *Commentary* 90.

of the Mosaic Law.

Jesus says, "It was said to those of ancient times, you shall not murder,... but I say to you..." (Mt 5.21-22). He teaches that anger leads to murder. Jesus has ignored the Psalmist who writes, "Refrain from anger, and forsake wrath" (Ps 37.8). In the rabbinic literature R. Eleazar says, "He who hates his brother belongs to the shedders of blood!"[17] Indeed, the LORD orders Moses to tell the people not to have hatred of their kin and to "love your neighbor as yourself" (Lv 19.17-18). Seneca says that anger is a temporary madness (*De Ira* 1.1.2). "Man is born for mutual aid; anger, for destruction..." (*De Ira* 1.5.2-3). Anger was a common topic in Roman schools.

Jesus says "you have heard that it was said, 'you shall not commit adultery.' But I say to you that everyone who looks at a woman with lust has already committed adultery with her in his heart" (Ex 20.14; Dt 5.18; Mt 5.27-20). (Apparently Jesus does not believe that women lust after men.) But Jews and pagans also condemned impure thought.[18] "He who has a pure heart in love, looks not on a woman with thoughts of fornication" (*Test. of Benjamin* 8.2).[19] Seneca condemns adulterous behavior by either husband or wife.[20] Aristotle writes, "What is a crime for a person to do, is a crime for a person to think..."[21] and Cicero asserts that lust is a powerful sin.[22]

The Jewish Jesus condemns Jews who divorce and remarry (Mt 5.31-32; 19.9), yet Dt 24.1ff clearly permits divorce and re-marriage, as does rabbinic law. Jesus incorrectly assumes that a Jewish woman, like a pagan woman, could initiate a divorce. The Stoic Musonius (ca 31-100 CE) condemned adultery, regarding marriage as sacred.[23]

Leviticus says that one should not swear falsely (19.12). Jesus says, "Do not swear at all" (Mt 5.33-37). *The Anchor Bible*

---

[17]Lachs, S., *Commentary* 91,94, DER XI.

[18]Lachs, S., *Commentary* 96-97.

[19]Lachs, S., *Commentary* 96-97.

[20]Motto, Anna Lydia, *Seneca*. (New York: Twayne Publishers, Inc., 1973), 60, Ep 94.26.

[21]Boring, M., HCNT, 58, #34, Magnum Moralia.

[22]Boring, M., HCNT, 58, #34, Goods and Evils 3.9.32 (LCL).

[23]Reale, Giovanni, Ed and Trans John R. Catan. *The History of Ancient Philosophy IV. The Schools of the Imperial Age* (State University of New York Press, 1990), 71.

Dictionary points out that Jesus' teachings on oaths, prayer, revenge, and marriage were close to the doctrines of the pagan Pythagoreans[24] who were also in favor of daily prayer (cf. Mt 6.9).

Quoting Scripture, Jesus preaches, "you have heard it was said, 'An eye for an eye and a tooth for a tooth.' But I say to you, Do not resist an evildoer. But if any one strikes you on the right cheek, turn the other also..." (Mt 5.38-39; Lk 6.29-30; cf. Ex 21.24f; Lv 24.20). Some Christian commentators still argue that the ethics of Jesus are loving and the ethics of Judaism are harsh and primitive. But compensation for injury was a common practice in the pagan world as it is today. Also, an eye for an eye was a vast improvement over the older tradition of a human life for an eye.[25]

The Lord commands the Jewish people to love their neighbors (Lev 19.18). Assuming Jesus means to include non-neighbors, he has achieved superiority only by ignoring the verse which appears at Lv 19.34 which says that "you shall love the stranger."[26] Jesus adds, "Love your enemies and pray for those who persecute you" (Mt 5.44; cf. Lk 6.27-28,32-36). Jesus does not mean that one should love one's enemy during combat, as some modern Christians think. As Gandhi and Martin Luther King have demonstrated, nonviolence under certain circumstances is effective, but this is not so if your persecutor is Hitler or the brutal Roman army. The early church was probably advocating that a Christian should react nonviolently when he or she is ostracized. In addition, Matthew is anachronistic since he refers to persecutions of Christians which did not occur until well after Jesus' death.

In the *Jewish Scriptures* one is commanded to treat one's enemies in a moral way; Jewish tradition teaches that if your enemy is hungry and thirsty, give him bread and water, etc. (see Ex 23.4-5; Dt 22.4; Prv 25.21).[27] The Qumranites express a hatred for the Sons of Darkness, i.e., those Jews and others who opposed the sect's understanding of God but this sect was not

---

[24]Freedman, David Noel. Ed. in Chief, *The Anchor Bible Dictionary*, 6 vols. (New York: Doubleday, 1992), vol. 5, 564.

[25]For more see Lachs, S., *Commentary* 103-104.

[26]Lachs, S., *Commentary* 107, 110 fn. 1.

[27]Lachs, S., *Commentary* 108, 111 fn. 12-14.

reflective of mainstream Judaism.

The idea that one should harm one's enemies and help one's friends was ancient. "Yet in the Greek world a different view gradually emerged when Pericles urged overcoming enemies by generosity and virtue."[28] The Stoics and Pythagoreans taught that one should behave toward one's enemies so that they will turn into friends.[29]

Jesus says, "whenever you give alms, do not sound a trumpet before you, as the hypocrites do in the synagogues and in the streets, so that they may be praised by others" (Mt 6.2). Giving alms on the street was common in both Jewish and pagan circles. As to sounding a trumpet in the synagogues or streets while giving to the poor, this nowhere appears in Jewish literature.[30]

Jesus directs his disciples to shut the door and pray in private to their hidden Father (Mt 6.6). So too, some pagan magicians advised their followers to pray in private, "to your hidden Father who sees that which is hidden."[31] None of the versions of the Lord's Prayer in Matthew and Luke are found in Jewish literature (Mk 11.25; Mt 6.9-15; Lk 11.2-4).

Jesus says, "Do not judge, so that you may not be judged" (Mt 7.1-5; Lk 6.37-38,41-42). But the idea that we should not judge others but rather should examine ourselves was a commonplace teaching among Stoic-Cynics like Seneca, as well as many other philosophers.

"Beware of false prophets, who come to you in sheep's clothing but inwardly are ravenous wolves" (Mt 7.15-20). Matthew is again anachronistic; he refers to Christian heretics or schismatics of his own time.

Golden Rule

Jesus preaches, "In everything do to others as you would have them do to you; for this is the law and the prophets" (Mt 7.12; Lk 6.31. Probably no saying of Jesus is more widely known among Christians than this "golden rule." Apologists even today use it

---

[28]Thucydides 4.19,1-4 as quoted in Fitzmyer, *Luke* vol 1 637, note on Lk 6.27.

[29]Diogenes Laertius 8.1,23 as quoted in Fitzmyer, Luke, vol 1, 637-38.

[30]Lachs, S., *Commentary* 112.

[31]Smith, M., *Magician*, 131. cp PGM XII, 265.

to demonstrate the superiority and uniqueness of Jesus' ethics over Jewish ethics, but it is hardly unique to Christianity. Consider, "You shall love your neighbor as yourself" (Lv 19.18); "And that which you hate, do to no man" (Tobit 4.15).[32] The golden rule is found in all the major religions of the world although the phrase Golden Rule is an 18th century label. It also appears in ancient Greek literature, e.g., "Isocrates, Nioles 61, 'Do not do unto others that which angers you when others do it to you.' Compare also Herodotus 3.142."[33]

J. Fitzmyer writes, "In antiquity many formulations, both positive and negative, were known."[34] He gives some examples of the rule:

- Lv 19.18 - "You must love your neighbor as yourself."

- Luke and Philo (20 BCE-50 CE) emphasize duty to God and humanity, to love God and man.[35]

- R. Hillel, a contemporary rabbi of Jesus, writes, "What is hateful to you, do not do to anyone else; that is the whole Law, all else is commentary. Go and learn."[36]

Calming the Storm: Mk 4.35-41

But let us return to Mark. Jesus and his disciples are in "the boat" which, along with other boats, is crossing the Sea of Galilee. (The other boats of vs. 36 probably originally served as witnesses to the storm miracle that follows this verse.)

Randel Helms points out in *Gospel Fictions*[37] that Matthew may have used both Jonah and the Psalmist in constructing this story. The Psalmist writes that when struck by a storm at sea, the crew and others, "cried to the LORD in their trouble [and] he made the storm be still, and the waves of the sea were hushed" (107.28-29). In Mark, the disciples wake Jesus who was apparently fatigued since he was sleeping during the storm! They cry

---

[32]Lachs, S., *Commentary* 143.

[33]Lachs, S., *Commentary* 144 fn. 6.

[34]Fitzmyer, J., *Luke*, vol 1, 639.

[35]Boring, M., HCNT, 128-129, #165.

[36]Fitzmyer, J., *Luke*, vol 1, 639, b. Sabbat 31a.

[37]Helms, Randel, *Gospel Fictions* (Buffalo: Prometheus Books, 1988), 76-81.

out to him in fear, asking him if he cares that they are perishing (Mk 4.38). Jesus commands the wind and the sea, "Peace! Be still!" and it is so (4.39).

Jonah 1.4-17 relates that the prophet is asleep on board a ship when God sends a storm, endangering the crew. They cry out in fear and pray to their gods to save them but to no avail. The captain wakes Jonah telling him to call on his God so that they might not perish. Jonah knows that it is because of his previous disobedience that God has sent the storm, and he tells the crew to throw him into the sea and the storm will cease. They do so and the storm ends. Jonah is swallowed by a fish; he prays and the Lord releases him. At last he obeys God's command to go to the pagan city of Nineveh in Mesopotamia, and tell them to desist from their evil behavior or else the city will be destroyed by God in forty days. The people of the great pagan city repent of their sins, God spares them, and all ends happily. Thus, God has reminded Jonah that God is responsible not only for Jews but for all people.

There are several parallels between Mark and Jonah. Jesus, like Jonah, is asleep when the storm endangers the boat (Mk 4.37-38; Jon 1.4-5). The disciples cry out in fear, asking Jesus if he cares that they might perish, as people do in Jonah (Mk 4.38; Jon 1.14). Jesus calms the sea (in Jonah, God does so) (Mk 4.39; Jon 1.15). Jesus criticizes the disciples for still having no faith (Mk 4.40), and Jonah was unfaithful when he disobeyed God. After three days in the fish, Jonah goes on to fulfill his mission to the pagans in Nineveh. In Mark, Jesus and his disciples finish the boat trip and arrive in the pagan country of the Gerasenes where Jesus exorcises a "legion" of demons from a pagan man, thus foreshadowing the church's mission to pagans.

Many miracles resulted ". . . from the virtues of Pythagoras." He predicted earthquakes and violent winds, and calmed the waves of rivers and seas so that his disciples could pass through the area (cf. Mt 8.26).[38] "Jesus himself accomplishes the mighty deed which is otherwise ascribed only to divine beings"[39] in the pagan world. In a story from Lucian, two of the divine sons of

---

[38]Martin, R., 173.
[39]Boring, M., HCNT, 66-67, Unit #54.

Zeus calm a similar storm.[40]   In Mark, Jesus sleeps during a dangerous storm; in Homer the hero sleeps on a dangerous battlefield (Iliad 4.223).   In both there are a storm and "help from the hero."[41]   "'Have pity,' I [Clitophon] wailed and cried, 'Lord Poseidon, and make a truce with us, the remnants of your shipwreck, we have already undergone many deaths through fear.'" (2nd century CE).[42] Poseidon was called "Lord" as is Jesus at Mt 8.25.   In pagan myth, a god or hero can control nature.[43] The gods calm storms to save sailors and other people, e.g., Aphrodite, Poseidon, Neptune.[44] The Dioscuri calmed the seas in the Homeric hymns.[45] The Egyptian goddess, Isis, is mistress of rivers, winds, and the sea, and calms the seas and brings on storms.[46]

---

[40]Ibid.
[41]Ibid.
[42]Boring, M., HCNT, 69, Unit #59.
[43]Cotter, W., Miracles, 131.
[44]Cotter, W., Miracles, 132ff.
[45]Cotter, W., Miracles, 134.
[46]Cotter, W., Miracles, #3.8, 136.

Chapter 4

Faithful Pagans

We decree and order that from now on, and for all time, Christians shall not eat or drink with Jews...
— Pope Eugenius IV Decree, 1442 CE

Demons and Pigs: Mk 5.1-20

Jesus and his disciples travel by boat to the eastern shore of the Sea of Galilee and disembark in the pagan region of Gerasa. Mark gives no reason for the trip. A pagan man who is possessed appears before Jesus. He has been living among the tombs, has broken his chains and is wandering about (Mk 5.2,8). He bows down and addresses Jesus, "Son of the Most High God... I adjure you by God do not torment me" (5.7). In Mark, this pagan is the only person to call Jesus *Son of God* other than the disciples. Jesus asks him who he is and the man replies, "My name is Legion; for we are many" (vs. 9). Mark's text switches from singular to plural, from *one* spirit to a *legion* of them. (Legion is the Roman military term for a unit of 4,000 to 6,000 soldiers.)

Once again we see that Jesus' knowledge is limited since he has to ask the demon who he is. The unclean spirits beg Jesus "not to send them out of the country" (vs. 10). Jesus doesn't exile them, but he outfoxes his foes by sending them into a nearby herd of about 2,000 pigs which rushes down a steep bank and drowns in the sea.

Would demons really fear being evicted from their "own country?" Would Jesus have permitted the demons to torment people in other areas? Mark's solution is to have Jesus send the demons into pigs which then drown in the sea. Even if the pigs die, is it possible for these supernatural entities to die? Luke attempts to correct this latter point by asserting that the demons feared going back "to the abyss" (Lk 8.31), but he apparently accepts the fact that demons were mortal.

Many scholars think that originally the story was located in a Jewish area. Mark, or his editor, knowing that Jews are forbidden to eat pork and so would not be raising pigs, placed the story in Gerasa. The name of this pagan area varies from manuscript to manuscript and gospel to gospel. Why was it so difficult to find a pagan region for the story? Because Mark relates that the demon-possessed pigs rushed down a steep bank into the sea and drowned, but there is no suitable bank or cliff bordering the Sea of Galilee. Mark and Luke placed the pigs near the city of Gerasa, but this is about 33 miles southeast of the Sea of Galilee.[1] Matthew locates the story in Gadara, but this is still about six miles from the sea.[2] Mark and parallels give no hint that the pigs ran a marathon, as E. Schweizer points out.[3]

The demons use God's name in begging Jesus to spare them but they would hardly make such use of God's name[4] which is why both Matthew and Luke omit this. Incidentally, why do the devils always speak Greek?

The former demoniac begs to be allowed to accompany Jesus who politely refuses his request and tells him to go home to his friends and tell them what the *Lord* has done for him (Mk 5.18-19). Mark says that the man told all the people what Jesus had done for him and they were amazed. Other than the blind beggar at Jericho, the only person who asks to follow Jesus is this man. This story was inserted by the early church to give scriptural support for the church's mission to pagans (non-Jews).[5]

Exorcisms are rare in ancient Judaism. There are none recorded in the *Jewish Scriptures*, and in the Mishnah (ca 200 CE) there are only three passages that assume the existence of demons, and none mention exorcism.[6]

---

[1]Fitzmyer, J., *Luke*, vol. 1, 736.
[2]Ibid.
[3]Schweizer, E., *Mark*, 113.
[4]Fitzmyer, J., *Luke*, vol 1., 738, vs. 28.
[5]Fitzmyer, J., *Luke*, vol 1. 735.
[6]Cotter, W., *Miracles*, 97-98.

Resurrection of Jairus' Daughter: Mk 5.21-43

Jesus crosses the sea in "the boat," returning to Galilee.

In Mark, Jesus raises only one person from the dead, the daughter of Jairus, the leader (5.22), or one of the leaders (5.38), of the synagogue. Jairus comes to Jesus, falls at his feet and repeatedly begs him to cure his dying daughter by the laying on of hands (Mk 5.22-23). Jesus heads for Jairus' house, accompanied by the father and a large crowd (5.24).

This is another sandwich story that is interrupted by an incident involving an unnamed woman who has been suffering from a hemorrhage for twelve years (Mk 5.25-34). Her faith is strong enough that she believes that if she only touches Jesus' clothes, she will be cured. She does so and the bleeding stops. Jesus knows immediately that power has gone out of him; he turns to the crowd, asking who touched his clothes. The woman falls down before him and explains "all that has happened" and Jesus says that her faith has cured her (Mk 5.34). Again we see that Jesus is not all -powerful or all-knowing since power leaves him and he has to ask who touched him. E. Schweizer concludes that this story is Mark's own composition.[7] The point of the story is again to show that Jewish religious leaders are impotent, i.e., Judaism is inefficacious.

A number of writers have interpreted this story as meaning that Jesus is superior to Jewish religious leaders in that he ignores Jewish ritual rules governing blood impurity. Mary D'Angelo disagrees, arguing that Jesus is not aware of the presence of blood[8] but she overlooks the fact that Jesus shows no concern even when he becomes aware that he has inadvertently violated a ritual law.[9]

E. Schweizer writes that "such miracles were attributed to pagan Greek wonder-workers..."[10] Arrian relates that the soldiers of Alexander the Great sought to touch his garment for healing. There are similar stories in Plutarch's *Life of Sulla* and Tacitus'

---

[7]Schweizer, E., *Mark*, 116.

[8]D'Angelo, Mary A. "(Re)Presentations of Women in the Gospels: John and Mark" pp 140-141 in Kraemer, Ross Shepard and Mary Rose D'Angelo, Eds., *Women and Christian Origins* (New York: Oxford University Press, 1999).

[9]Compare pagan purity rituals before entering temple, Boring, M., HCNT, 210, #303.

[10]Schweizer, E., *Mark*, 121.

Histories.[11]

Pagan gods helped women, too. In an inscription from Epidaurus, a god helps a woman named Cleo deliver a baby after a pregnancy of five years. We can accept the gestation period, but we have some difficulty with the idea that after his birth, the infant immediately washes himself at the fountain and walks about with his mother![12]

While Jesus is talking to the healed woman, some people from Jairus' house exclaim that his daughter is dead. Jesus allows "no one to follow him [to the house] except Peter, James, and John, the brother of James" (Mk 5.37). (Where did the disciples come from? The flow of the narrative is smooth if one omits vs. 37. Apparently the disciples have been added to the original story.)

Jesus enters Jairus' home and says, "The child is not dead, but sleeping" (Mk 5.39). The mourners scoff, and Jesus puts everyone outside the house except the child's parents and the three disciples. He takes the child's hand and commands her to get up. She rises and walks around. Mark says *they* were amazed (Mk 5.42). Jesus then forbids them to tell anyone what has occurred (the messianic secret again), and orders someone to feed the girl.

The tale of the raising of Jairus' daughter is very much like the standard pagan healing story:

- a person has an ailment;

- the sick person or a relative or friend begs the hero for a cure;

- the hero cures the person by touch, spittle, or words; and

- proof is provided that the cure was effective, e.g., Jairus' daughter gets up, walks around, and is given food to eat.

Often Mark and the other evangelists will use a pagan story but clothe it with details taken from the Jewish Scriptures. R. Helms compares the Synoptic story about Jairus' daughter with the

---

[11]Boring, M., HCNT, 78, #74.
[12]Martin, F., 225.

prophet Elisha's resurrection of a young boy 2 Kgs 4.18-37; Mk 5.21-43). He observes five points of similarity.[13] In both stories:

- a parent begs the hero to come and save his or her child who is near death;

- on the way to the child the hero receives a message not to come since the child is dead, though this deters neither Jesus nor Elisha;

- both healers turn people out of the house where the child lies;

- in each story the hero touches the child, speaks, and the child awakes;

- finally, in Mark and 2 Kings the crowds or the parents of the resurrected child are amazed.

Excursus: Luke's Resurrection at Nain

R. Helms also finds[14] five points of similarity between Elijah in 1 Kings 17.10,17-24 and Luke 7.11-17:

- Both begin with the words, "And it came to pass."

- In each the hero meets a woman at the gate of a city.

- Both magic workers speak and touch the woman's dead son who rises and speaks.

- The miracle establishes that each of the heroes is a prophet.

- Both end with the same words, "he gave him to his mother."

Helms writes that what is "striking is that all the gospel stories of Jesus' resurrecting a dead loved one are based on the resurrections..."[15] performed by Elijah and Elisha in 1 and 2 Kings. We would point out that there is one significant difference between the stories of Jesus and Elijah and that is that the

---

[13]Helms, R., 65-66.

[14]Helms, R., 64.

[15]Helms, R., 64.

Jewish prophet prays to the Lord for help in restoring the boy to life (1 Kgs 17.20,22). The Messiah, Jesus, never names God as the source of power for his miraculous deeds. This is very non-Jewish.

Resurrections were not common among pagan magicians, but in the *Jewish Scriptures* they are even rarer.[16] Pagans could misinterpret signs of death in a patient, as when Asclepiades meets a funeral procession and ascertains that the man is still alive.[17] J. Fitzmyer states that resurrection stories appear in the pagan works of Pliny and Apuleius, as well as other writings.[18] In Philostratus' biography of the Jesus-like figure, Apollonius of Tyana (d ca 96 CE), Apollonius stops a funeral bier, touches the dead girl, and wakes her from death. He then returns her to the house of her father.[19]

According to Apuleius, the Greek god of healing, Asclepius, raised a man thought dead.[20] And Malodorous writes that when Alcestis died, she was brought back from the dead by Hercules.[21] The resurrected Jesus, like Hercules and Dionysius, descends to the land of the dead (prison) and rescues spirits from Hades (1 Pet 3.18-19).

Rejection in Jesus' Hometown: Mk 6.1-6

Jesus teaches on the Sabbath in the synagogue of his hometown which remains unknown. Mark uses the word "Nazareth" five times in his gospel, but not here in this story. Jesus' (former) neighbors ask, "Is not this the carpenter, the son of Mary and brother of James and Joses and Judas and Simon, and are not his sisters here with us?" (Mk 6.3). A Jewish child's ancestry would not be traced solely through the mother, since this could imply that she had borne an illegitimate child, an insult to both mother and child. Matthew corrects this by adding that Jesus is "the son of the carpenter" (Mt 13.55).

In Mark and Matthew Jesus' listeners in the synagogue are

---

[16]Smith, M., *Magician*, 118.

[17]Boring, M., HCNT,79, #76.

[18]In what follows, see J. Fitzmyer, *Commentary on Luke*, vol 1, 656-658.

[19]Boring, M., HCNT, 203-204, #290.

[20]Martin, F., 179.

[21]Martin, F., 214.

astounded at his teachings and his "deeds of power" (Mk 6.2), and yet turn against him. Apparently they think that wisdom should not issue from a person with the low social status of a carpenter (Mk 6.2-3), but they knew his status before he spoke. Why the change of heart? Philostratus, writing in the 3rd century CE, states that Apollonius of Tyana said, "Other men regard me as the equal of the gods, and some of them even as a god, but until now my own country alone ignores me..."[22] Plutarch and Dio Chrysostom write of similar tales of rejection of philosophers in their own countries.[23]

According to Mark, the faith of the Jews in the synagogue is so defective that Jesus *could* not perform any miracles in his hometown, except for the healing of a few sick people by the laying on of hands (Mk 6.5). Matthew rehabilitates Jesus by asserting that Jesus did not do *many* miracles there, and Luke omits any hint that Jesus' power is limited.

The rejection at Nazareth is the first story of Jesus' ministry that Luke records. By placing it at the beginning of his gospel he seeks to depict Jesus as a teacher, not merely the miracle monger of Mark's gospel. In the synagogue, Jesus reads from the scroll of Isaiah, indicating that he (the Messiah) is a champion of the oppressed, the captives, the poor, and the blind, although as we said before, there is no such messianic tradition in Judaism.

Luke adds two significant items to the accounts of Mark and Matthew: First, the people identify Jesus as "Joseph's" son (Lk 4.22), rather than as a carpenter (Mark) or the son of the carpenter (Mt 13.54-55). Second, unlike Mark and Matthew, the audience takes no offense at Jesus' humble status. Instead, in Luke Jesus teaches that there was a severe famine in Israel, and Elijah (ca 850 BCE) was sent by God to help a pagan widow of Sidon by multiplying food. In like manner, the prophet's disciple, Elisha, cleanses only the pagan leper, Naaman the Syrian, although there were many Jewish lepers in Israel. In response to Jesus' pro-pagan message, the people in the synagogue attempt to kill Jesus by throwing him off the top of a hill.

Luke has begun his account of Jesus' ministry with an old pagan slander, namely that Jews hated non-Jews.

---

[22]Boring, M., HCNT, 96, #106.
[23]Ibid.

Jesus Sends Out the Twelve: Mk 6.6b-13

Jesus teaches in the villages of Galilee (Mk 6.6b), and then sends the twelve out ". . . two by two..." (Mk 6.7), as does the early church (see Acts). Jesus gives his disciples typical Cynic instructions: they are not to take any possessions with them except a staff, one pair of sandals and a single tunic (Mk 6.8-9). Also, they are to take no bread, no bag, and no money, and they are to exorcise unclean spirits and proclaim repentance.

Plutarch reports that holy men took no wallet and no food on their journeys since they "devote all their time to god."[24] Diogenes (2nd century CE), says that the Cynics took only one cloak, a wallet and a staff when they traveled.[25] The Stoic, Musonius Rufus (d 100 CE), relates that wearing one cloak is better than two and it is best to wear no sandals.[26] The editors of HCNT write that there are "numerous analogies between Cynic wandering philosophers and early Christian wandering missionaries..."[27]

To whom are the apostles sent? Mark implies that their mission is to Jews in Galilee and Matthew spells this out. Jesus commands the disciples to "Go nowhere among the gentiles, and enter no town of the Samaritans, but go rather to the lost sheep of the house of Israel" (Mt 10.5-6). Some apologists erroneously use this text as "a proof" that Jesus, being Jewish, naturally dislikes non-Jews.

This pericope is anti-Jewish. In Mark, Jesus says that if (Jewish) towns refuse to welcome or listen to the twelve, they are to leave and "shake off the dust that is on [their] feet as a testimony against them" (Mk 6.11). Matthew is more explicit than Mark. He adds that for any (Jewish) town that rejects the disciples, ". . . it will be more tolerable for the land of Sodom and Gomorrah on the day of judgment than for that town" (Mt 10.15-16).

After Mark's long account of the death of John the Baptist (Mk 6.14-29), the disciples abruptly reappear, reporting to Jesus "all that they had done and taught" (Mk 6.30). E. Schweizer asserts that this verse was added by Mark or his editors.[28] Matthew

---

[24]Boring, M., HCNT, 80, #79.

[25]Boring, M., HCNT, 81, #80.

[26]Boring, M., HCNT, 81-82, #81.

[27]Boring, M., HCNT, 118, #144; also see #148,296,298,453.

[28]Schweizer, E., *Mark*, p 135.

never reports that the disciples returned to Jesus; they just appear in the grain field story at Mt 12.1ff. This is another story added by the early church to support missionary efforts.

Death of John the Baptist: Mk 6.14-29

According to Mark, Jesus' fame has spread throughout Galilee. Herod Antipas and others think that Jesus is John the Baptist raised from the dead (thus Jesus is able to do miracles). Still others think Jesus is Elijah, or a prophet like those of long ago.

Mark relates that John the Baptist is beheaded by Herod (Antipas), the Tetrarch who ruled Galilee under Roman authority (Mark wrongly calls him king). Mark relates that Herod married the ex-wife of his brother Philip, Tetrarch of Etruria. The Baptist condemns this union of Herod and Herodias. Because of this condemnation, Herodias desires the death of the Baptist. When her daughter's dance at a banquet pleased Herod, she is granted a favor, and her mother asks for the head of John the Baptist. Herod agrees and, despite his "deep grief," orders the "holy man" beheaded (Mk 6.26,20) and delivers his head on a platter. Note that the execution of the Jewish prophet "is given without any exaltation of the martyr."[29] However, exaltation of the martyr is typical of later Christian Martyrologies.

Many scholars hold this story of John's death to be unhistorical. It contains a number of errors. E. Schweizer mentions a few:[30]

- Philip the Tetrarch was not married to Herodias, but rather to her daughter, Salome.

- Josephus, the first-century CE Jewish historian, gives a different cause for John's death: John had a large following and Herod Antipas feared an insurrection (*Ant* 18.5.116-119).

- Josephus writes that the death of John took place at the fortress Machaerus, east of the Dead Sea. One problem is that the guests, high officials and leading citizens of Galilee,

---

[29]Schweizer, E., *Mark*, p 134.
[30]Schweizer, E., *Mark*, p 132-34.

would not fit into this small fort. The party would have had to be held at the Herodian palace in Tiberius, the capital of Galilee. Neither Mark nor Matthew relates where the banquet was held.

- Schweizer writes that, "it is almost inconceivable that the princess would dance in this way..."[31] We would add that John's head being delivered on a platter during a formal banquet is also inconceivable!

Some scholars think the section of Josephus dealing with John's death is a Christian interpolation. They think the relevant passage in *Antiquities* (18.116-119)[32] disturbs the narrative flow. King Aretas is angry because Herod Antipas divorced his daughter to marry Philip's ex-wife and so declares war on Herod. Then Josephus discusses war tactics. The passage about John follows, after which Josephus returns to the war plans. On the other hand, other scholars believe that John was an historical Jewish figure, and that only the reference to John's baptizing, although not for the remission of sins, was added by Christian editors. These scholars see John as an historical figure, but having no connection with Jesus.

Feeding 5,000 & 4,000: Mk 6.32-44; 8.1-9

In Galilee, Jesus feeds 5,000 men with five loaves and two fish, twelve baskets of food are left over (Mk 6.32-44). (Mt 14.21 says 5,000 men plus women and children.) Later, in pagan territory, the Marcan Jesus feeds 4,000 men with seven loaves and a few fish, with seven baskets of food left over (Mk 8.1-10; Mt 15.32-39).

R. Helms argues persuasively that the feeding stories are based on 2 Kings 4.42-44,[33] where Elisha feeds 100 hungry people with only 20 loaves and a sack of grain with food left over. Jesus is more powerful than Elisha; he feeds more people with less food. The Jewish prophet fulfills the Lord's will; Jesus again acts on his own authority.

---

[31] Schweizer, E., *Mark*, p 132.
[32] Boring, M., HCNT, 96-97, #107.
[33] Helms, R., 75.

Some apologists argue that Jesus here shows "compassion" for the Jewish crowd, because they are "like sheep without a shepherd" (Mk 6.34), but Jesus is again condemning the Jewish people's religious leaders as inferior to himself and inefficacious.

At Mk 6.37, the disciples ask Jesus if they should "buy 200 *denarii* worth of bread..." and give it to the people to eat. A single *denarius* was equivalent to a laborer's pay for one day,[34] so 200 *denarii* would be the wages for a person for about seven months. Where did Jesus and the disciples get this much money? They don't beg. We get no hint from Mark until much later (Mk 15.40), when we learn that women provided for Jesus while he was in Galilee. According to many scholars, the feeding stories prefigure the institution of the Eucharist at the Last Supper.[35] Although pagan magicians do not multiply food, they are commonly pictured as providing it.[36]

Excursus: Miracle at Cana Jn 2.1-10

Pausanias[37] assures us there were many witnesses who verified that at the festival of Dionysius, three empty pots behind locked doors were miraculously filled with wine. So too, Jesus attends a wedding in Cana of Galilee where there are many witnesses. When the wine runs out, Jesus has six jars filled with water, each holding about 20 or 30 gallons. He turns the water to wine, which is witnessed by the steward when he tastes the water (Jn 2.9). This is one-up-manship. The Dionysian story has witnesses, three pots, and the miracle occurs behind locked doors. Jesus has witnesses, six *large* jars, and the miracle occurs in the sight of all. Jesus' wine was also the best wine. Did the guests drink 120 gallons of wine or more? This story is used by apologists to argue that Jesus approved of marriage, but the early gospels know nothing of it.

---

[34]Throckmorton, Jr., Burton H., Ed., *Gospel Parallels*, (Nashville: Thomas Nelson Publishers, 1992), 90, fn j.

[35]Schweizer, E., *Mark*, 138.

[36]Martin, F., 215.

[37]Martin, F., 215.

Walking on Water: Mk 6.47-52

When the evening comes, Jesus goes alone to "a mountain" to pray. The disciples are in a boat on the Sea (of Galilee) heading for Bethsaida, although they will not arrive there until two chapters later at Mk 8.22.[38] Early in the morning, Jesus returns from the mountain to the sea, and sees that his disciples are in the middle of the sea having a hard time rowing the boat against the wind. Jesus appears walking on the water, "intending to pass them by" (vs. 48). Could Jesus see a ship in distress from the shore, several miles away? If Jesus wanted to rescue the disciples, why does Mark say that he intended to pass them by?

The disciples are terrified when they see Jesus, fearing that he is a ghost. Jesus reassures them, enters the boat, and the wind ceases (Mk 6.50-51). Mark says that the disciples are utterly astounded since "they did not understand about the [multiplication of the] loaves, but their hearts were hardened" (Mk 6.51-52, cf. Mk 8.17). Mark hates the Pharisees and he here equates the disciples with outsiders who are to be damned to hell!

Matthew adds that Peter also walks on the water. Heading toward Jesus, Peter becomes terrified and begins to sink (Mt 14.30). Jesus rescues him. But Matthew ameliorates this faithlessness of Peter and the others by omitting Mark's comment about their "hearts being hardened" (Mk 6.52) and by having the disciples worship Jesus, declaring him to be "the Son of God" (Mt 14.33).

In the *Jewish Scriptures*, God (and sometimes prophets like Moses, Elijah, and Elisha) miraculously control the seas and rivers[39] (cf. Job 9.8). "You trample the sea with your horses" (cf. Hab 3.15).[40] "The Lord tramples the waves of the sea" (cf. Job 9.6-11).[41] The Lord makes a way on the seas.[42]

E. Schweizer writes that "Greek writers asserted that super-

---

[38]Schweizer, E., *Mark*, 142.

[39]Fitzmyer, J., *Luke*, vol 1, 728.

[40]Cotter, W., *Miracles*, 149.

[41]Cotter, W., #3.31, 149-150.

[42]Cotter, W., #3.33, 150.

men and demons could walk upon the sea."[43] One of Poseidon's sons, Orion, walked on the sea as if it were solid ground.[44] Plutarch, Menander, Strabo, and even the Jewish historian, Josephus, wrote of how Alexander the Great crossed the inlet of the Pamphylian Sea, sometimes indicating that a miracle occurred.[45] Josephus sees Alexander's crossing the Sea as miraculous (the water is held back for him), but he states that everyone is welcome to their own opinion.[46] Pagans presupposed "that divine origin is demonstrated by great deeds. This conception is significant for the composition of the Gospels as a whole, especially for the idea of Jesus' divine sonship."[47] Great deeds indicate divinity of the one who performs them.

Mk 6.53-56 relates that the boat with Jesus and his disciples came to shore at Gennesaret in Galilee. At once people recognize Jesus and bring their sick to him. The people had come from the villages, cities and farms and all who touched the fringe of his cloak were cured. E. Schweizer attributes this summary statement to Mark's pen.[48]

Condemning Oral Law: Pharisees and Scribes

We must now look at Jesus' attitude toward oral law (and sometimes written law) and its defenders. "Among Orthodox Jews, it is believed that both the written and the oral (unwritten) laws were given to Moses on Mt. Sinai."[49] Rabbinical interpretations of the written law were collected and published in the Mishnah ca 200 CE by Judah ha Nasi. The discussions of the Mishnah are contained in the Talmuds, "*The Jerusalem Talmud* was compiled in the late 5th Century (CE) and *The Babylonian Talmud* in the late 6th Century (CE)..."[50]

In Mark Chapter 7, Jesus condemns "the Pharisees" and "some scribes" who have popped up from Jerusalem. Pharisees did not

---

[43]Schweizer, E., *Mark*, 141.

[44]Boring, M., HCNT, 99, #111.

[45]Martin, F., 157-158.

[46]Martin, F., 157-158.

[47]Boring, M., HCNT, 96, #105.

[48]Schweizer, E., *Mark*, 143.

[49]Cohn-Sherbok, Lavinia and Dan, *A Popular Dictionary of Judaism*, (1995), (Chicago: NTC Publishing Group, 1997), 130.

[50]Cohn-Sherbok, L., 174.

live in Galilee at this time and Mark treats scribes as if they were a unified political, social, or religious block, but they are not depicted in this way by Josephus.

The Pharisees and scribes observe that some of Jesus' disciples are eating without ritually washing their hands (Mk 7.2). Mark flatly states that "all the Jews, do not eat unless they thoroughly wash their hands..." (vs. 3), and they observe many other rituals concerning cups and pots, etc. (vs. 4). The Pharisees and scribes criticize Jesus, asking why his disciples do not live "according to the tradition of the elders..." (vs. 5), as if oral law was not from God.

Lachs writes, "The earliest reference to this practice [of the ritual washing of hands] in Jewish sources is the Mishnah (ca 200 CE) (M. Ber. 8.2-4)."[51] Montefiore states that this practice in Jesus' time applied only to priests; laypersons and the pupils of the rabbis were exempt.[52] R. Bultmann states that this account "has all the characteristics of pure polemic of the early church."[53] Beck asserts that Mk 7.6-13 is "vitriolic anti-Jewish polemic."[54]

Jesus quotes Isaiah who writes that God commanded him to tell Jews, "This people honors me with their lips, but their hearts are far from me; in vain do they worship me..." (Mk 7.6-7; Mt 15.8-9; cf. Isa 29.13). As we said above, Mark does not relate the fact that Isaiah chastises the Israelites (the northern kingdom) but intends no permanent condemnation of them or Jews in general.

Jesus condemns the oral law, "You abandon the commandment of God and hold to human tradition" (Mk 7.8; cf. Mt 15.6). In Matthew, too, Jesus sees oral law as human, "in vain do they worship me, teaching human precepts as doctrines" (Mk 15.9). As we said above, in Judaism, all law, oral or written, is believed to come from God.

Pagans, too, placed divine law above human law. Plutarch writes that we are in the world "to obey the commands of the gods"[55] (cf. Mk 7.8). Epictetus (55-135 CE) asks, should we

---

[51]Lachs, S., *Commentary*, 246.

[52]Ibid.

[53]As quoted in Beck, N., *Mature Christianity*, 151.

[54]Beck, N., *Mature Christianity*, 151-152.

[55]Boring, M., HCNT, 57, #31.

obey human laws, "these wretched laws of ours, the laws of the dead, and... not [look] to the laws of the Gods...?"[56] A number of pagan writers condemned Jewish law as Jesus does here (see Chapter 9).

Jesus goes on to say that the Pharisees and scribes do not honor their parents because they set aside money (*corban*) for the temple (see Ex 20.12; 21.17; Dt 5.16; Lv 20.9), and Jesus adds that this robs their parents of support (Mk 7.8-11). *Corban* was money put in trust for the temple, but this does not mean that Jews were free to starve their parents any more than it would under today's law. Matthew drops this.

Mk 7.19b is often used to show that Jesus rejected Jewish food laws. Mark says that Jesus "declared all foods clean." But this verse is missing from the earliest extant manuscript of Mark, the third-century CE P[45], and does not appear in Mark until the manuscripts of the 4th and 5th centuries. It is a scribal gloss (a comment written in the margin of a manuscript and incorporated into the text by a later copyist.).

Here are some comments on the statement of Mark as to Jesus "declaring" all foods as clean:

- Most scholars consider Mk 7.19b to be a late insertion.

- Some think that Jesus is depicted as abandoning ritual law, at least the food laws of the *Jewish Scriptures* and oral law, but if Jesus had abandoned any of the fundamental elements of Judaism, one could hardly blame Jews and Jewish leaders for rejecting Jesus' claim to be a Jewish Messiah, prophet, or teacher. And why would he have a large Jewish following?

- The New Jerusalem Bible asserts that possibly the phrase was a scribal gloss.[57]

- We do not know where Jesus and his disciples are dining, except that it is somewhere in Galilee. Are his enemies, the Pharisees and scribes, dining with Jesus? The disciples make no response to what would be an extremely controversial teaching. This story appears to be a late addition.

---

[56]Reale, G., 86.
[57]Wansbrough, H., *The New Jerusalem Bible*, 1671, fn f.

Dinner with "Gentiles"

Christian scholars are inaccurate in picturing Jews as exclusive in refusing to eat with non-Jews. Jewish extra-biblical literature clearly indicates that Jews ate with non-Jews.

In Acts of the Apostles, Peter explicitly says to his first pagan converts, Cornelius and his household, "You... know that it is unlawful for a Jew to associate with or visit a Gentile." God, however, has shown Peter that he "should not call anyone profane or unclean" (Acts 10.28). There was and is no Jewish law forbidding contact between Jews and non-Jews, not in the *Jewish Scriptures*, the works of Philo or Josephus, nor any mainstream Jewish writing.

This passage shows a misunderstanding of Jewish law. It is not *people* who are unclean. Rather, ritual laws are to be followed when a person is in an impure *condition*. Generally, only Jews can cause other Jews to be in a state of impurity, and the remedy for the condition of ritual impurity was generally minor — immersion in water and waiting until sunset. Most ritual rules in the *Jewish Scriptures* normally applied only to the priests and others intending to enter the temple. E. Haenchen is right when he writes, "diaspora Jews were not hermetically sealed off from dealings with the Gentiles..."[58] Pagans, too, had a huge number of ritual rules, but this did not stop them from associating with pagans with different rules, nor with Jesus.

There is no external support for Acts 10.28 until Irenaeus (ca 180 CE).[59] Cyprian (d 270 CE) refers to "calling no man unclean"[60] but he does not cite 10.28a which refers to the alleged Jewish law.

The Marcan Jesus' anti-Jewish diatribe ends with a long list of sins attributed to the human heart: fornication, theft, murder, adultery, avarice, wickedness, envy, slander, and pride (Mk

---

[58]Haenchen, Ernst, *The Acts of the Apostles: A Commentary*, Trans. from the 14th German edition (1965), revised by R. McL. Wilson (Philadelphia: The Westminster Press, 1971.), 350, fn 4.

[59]*Ante-Nicene Fathers: Translations of The Writings of the Fathers down to A.D. 325* (ANF), Editors, The Rev. Alexander Roberts, D.D., and James Donaldson, LL.D, American Reprint of the Edinburgh Edition, 10 vols (Grand Rapids: Wm. B. Eerdman's Publishing Company, Reprinted May 1987), Irenaeus, Against Heresies, Bk 3.12.

[60]ANF, Cyprian, Epistle 58.5.

7.21-22). Pagans also supplied long lists of invective against their opponents. Dio Cocceianus (1st cent. CE) described his opponents as "...ignorant,... evil-spirited,... impious,... liars and deceivers,... preaching for the sake of gain and glory...."[61]

Syrophoenician Woman: Mk 7.24-30

Jesus' first trip to pagan territory is in Mark Chapter 5. He makes his only other trip into pagan territory at 7.24-9.29.

Only the first two gospels, Mark and Matthew, have the story of the Syrophoenician woman. Mark relates that Jesus, wanting to be alone, went to the region of Tyre (southern Syria NW of Galilee). As soon as he enters one of Mark's pop-up houses, a Syrophoenician woman having heard about him, instantly comes to the house begging Jesus "to cast the demon out of her daughter..." who is at home (Mk 7.26).

Jesus says to the pagan woman, "Let the children be fed first, for it is not fair to take the children's food and throw it to the dogs [non-Jews]" (Mk 7.27). To which the woman replies that even the dogs are allowed to eat the children's crumbs (vs. 28). Jesus admires her witty response and announces that the demon has left her daughter. Mark tells us that at home she found that this was so (vss 29-30).

Matthew is unhappy that in Mark the woman's wit is what saves the child, so he attributes the exorcism to the woman's faith (Mt 15.28). (Also, In Matthew the woman is a Canaanite, though they no longer existed in the time of Jesus.)

The pagan woman's faith is very strong, as is the faith of all other pagans in the Synoptics (including Pontius Pilate, in that he testifies to Jesus' innocence).

Additional stories involving the strong faith of pagans were added by Matthew and Luke. For instance, in Matthew a centurion comes to ask Jesus to heal his paralyzed servant. Jesus says to the pagan, "Truly I tell you, in *no one* in Israel have I found such faith" (Mt 8.10; cf. Lk 7.9). Jesus adds that many non-Jews will enter the kingdom "while the heirs of the kingdom [Jews] will be thrown into the outer darkness, where there will be weeping and gnashing of teeth" (Mt 8. 11-12).

---

[61]Boring, M., HCNT, 132, #169.

Some Christian apologists argue that ancient Jews hated non-Jews and use this passage about the dogs as evidence that Jesus, being a "typical Jew," was prejudiced against non-Jews. But Jesus' bias against pagans is a creation of the early church. It is contradicted by the fact that Jesus cures the pagan woman's daughter and, according to Matthew, it is because of her "faith." The gospel writers had a bias *in favor* of non-Jews not against them. In the Matthean birth scene, the pagan magi (wise men) are the first to pay homage to the baby Jesus (Mt 2.11). In Mark and Matthew a Roman centurion at the foot of the cross identifies Jesus as "God's Son." Indeed, Jesus has come to save "gentiles" though their salvation will not begin until after Jesus' death.

Healing a Deaf and Mute Man: Mk 7.31-37

Jesus leaves the area of Tyre and travels north through Sidon and then back southeast to the area of the Ten Cities, or Decapolis. Mark is ignorant of Palestinian geography; one would not go north to reach the south. Matthew omits the reference.

A deaf and mute man begs Jesus for a cure; Jesus takes him away from the crowd, puts his fingers in the man's ears and touches the man's tongue with spit (Mk 7.33). In this story, Jesus uses common pagan magical techniques. In Mark, Jesus commands "them" not to tell anyone who helped them, but they spread the news anyway. Matthew omits Jesus' secrecy order. He also omits the magical procedures and the whole story is omitted by Luke and John.

Chapter 5

The Messiah and the Son of Man

Jesus asked his disciples, "Who do you say that I am?" Peter answered, "You are the Messiah."
— Mark 8.29

The place of origin of the myth [of the 'son of man'] is not to be sought in Iran, or in Judea or even in Ugarit, but in the German universities.
— Paul Winter

Jesus leaves pagan territory by boat and crosses the sea to the district of Dalmanutha (Mk 8.10) where "the Pharisees" pop up and ask Jesus "for a sign from heaven" (Mk 8.11). Jesus insists that no sign will be given "to this generation," i.e., to the Jewish people (Mk 8.12). Matthew has "evil and adulterous generation" (16.4) and his Jesus asserts that no sign will be given except the sign of Jonah, referring to the prophet who spent three days in the belly of a fish. Matthew this as a prophecy of Jesus' resurrection on the third day. This is an allusion foreshadowing Jesus' death, which Matthew and Luke have added to prove that Jesus is conscious of God's plan and willingly accepts it.

Spiritual Blindness of Disciples: Mark 8.14-21

The Marcan Jesus and his disciples are re-crossing the sea, returning to the Decapolis. He warns his disciples to beware of the

73

yeast of the Pharisees and of Herod, that is, their false teachings. The disciples are worried as they think that Jesus is referring to real bread, and they only have one loaf left in the boat.

Jesus, reading the disciples' minds, denounces them for their spiritual blindness, saying that their hearts are hardened, that they have eyes and ears but do not see or hear (Mk 8.14-21).

Matthew continues to rehabilitate the disciples; they are *not* blind and *do* understand the significance of Jesus' saying about the yeast (Mt 16.12). The early church created this incident to combat false heretical teachings that plagued the early church.

Jesus and his disciples disembark at Bethsaida in pagan territory. Jesus secretly escorts a pagan blind man out of a village, puts spittle on the man's eyes and lays hands on them. The man perceives people as trees. A second touch cures him entirely. Dio Cassius relates that the Emperor Vespasian was magnified by heaven when he cured a blind man using spittle,[1] and healed a blind man with a withered hand.[2] In Mark, for all practical purposes Jesus' ministry ends at this point. Matthew and Luke see that this story indicates that Jesus' power was limited, and they omit it.

Compare Jesus' ministry in Mark with a papyrus as described by M. Smith. Here is what a spirit can do for a pagan wonder worker: (It) sends dreams and calms the wild beasts; it raises up winds from the earth and restrains the foam of the sea. The spirit exorcises many evil demons, and is able to bring down stars as in Mk 13.25.[3]

Peter's Declaration: Mk 8.27-30

The Jewish people do not understand who Jesus is or why he has come. The following incident makes this clear. Jesus and his disciples are on the way to the pagan region of the city of Caesarea Philippi in the Decapolis. Jesus asks his disciples, "Who do people say that I am?" (Mk 8.27). They answer that some people think that he is John the Baptist, others that he is Elijah, and still others think that he is one of the prophets. Peter is asked who he thinks Jesus is. The chief disciple answers,

---

[1]Martin, F., 166.

[2]Ibid.

[3]Smith, M., *Magician*, 130-131.

"You are the Messiah" (Mk 8.29), the other disciples apparently concur. Mark, Matthew and Luke again bring in the messianic secret; the disciples are not to tell anyone about Jesus.

Plutarch writes about the hidden identity and divine powers attributed to Romulus, the co-founder of Rome.[4] He also quotes Homer, "No god am I; why likenest thou me to the immortals?"[5] The HCNT editors state that, "Among enlightened Greeks the tradition of rejecting divine predications about human beings was widespread,"[6] which is why the Synoptic Jesus never explicitly identifies himself as a god.

The status of the disciples in Mark is further elevated by Matthew when he changes Peter's response from, "the Messiah," to "the Messiah, the Son of the living God" (Mt 16.16). Jesus blesses Peter saying that he has received this from God, not from men (Mt 16.17). The trouble with this is that the disciples have already addressed Jesus as "the Son of God" after Jesus walked on water (Mt 14.33), and there Jesus made no response. M. Smith informs us that pagan magicians sometimes identified themselves as "the Son of the living God."[7]

In Matthew, Jesus not only praises the chief disciple for his answer, but he miraculously predicts that Peter will found the future church, "You are Peter and upon this rock I will build my church" (Mt. 16.18). (In church tradition, Peter was the first bishop of Rome.) Jesus also says the church will have the keys to let people into the kingdom of heaven. In some pagan myths heaven is locked, and keys are needed to enter. Virtually all critical scholars agree that these rock and key sayings came from the early church.

Benefiting as many people as possible was the principal task of the divine man. He cured people and, after his death, his disciples passed on his teachings, benefiting future generations. Philo saw Moses in this way, as others saw various kings, generals, and philosophers. And so early Christians saw Jesus.

Pythagorean philosophy was "understood as a divine revelation..."[8] Their founder was seen "not so much as a perfect man

---

[4]Boring, M., HCNT, 95, #104.
[5]Boring, M., HCNT, 104, #120.
[6]Boring, M., HCNT, 105, #120
[7]Smith, M., *Magician*, 165.
[8]Reale, G., 249.

but as a Daimon or God or, more generally, a prophet or a superior human being who is in contact with the Gods."[9] A fragment attributed to Empedocles (5th century BCE) states, "But I go about [among] you as an immortal God, no longer as a mortal...." The philosopher relates that when he goes to men and women, "I am honored by them... they follow after me... in their thousands, to learn..." some seeking wisdom and others seeking healing.[10] Unusual here is that Empedocles, himself, claims that he is a god. In the ancient world, some followers thought of a philosopher as divine, but the individual himself usually did not claim to be divine, did not "grasp at divinity." Bad emperors, like Caligula, were severely criticized for making such claims.

Excursus: Messiah and the Son of Man

Messiah

In Hebrew, *messiah* refers to an anointed one (Greek Christos). In the *Jewish Scriptures*, *messiah* is applied to priests, kings and prophets of Israel, and even to one pagan, the Persian king Cyrus who freed Jews from captivity in Babylonia. A messiah is one who serves God's purposes; he is an instrument of God. After the fall of Israel (both the northern and southern kingdoms), a future Messiah was expected who would restore the kingdom and usher in the reign of God. But is "the Messiah" of the *Christian Scriptures* compatible with the Jewish concept of Messiah? Was this idea derived from Judaism?

The Messiah is an anthology edited by James H. Charlesworth in 1992. In his own contribution, he correctly asserts that Matthew's concept of "the Messiah" was not Jewish,[11] nor was the belief that there was a widespread expectation of a coming Messiah. Jesus did not fulfill Jewish messianic prophecies.[12] Charlesworth says that the idea that Jesus is *the* Messiah who is put to death by Jews is anti-Jewish.[13] He concludes that messianic

---

[9]Ibid.

[10]Boring, M., HCNT, 171, #229.

[11]Charlesworth, J., *The Messiah*, 4, referring to Wikenhauser, Alfred, *New Testament Introduction* Trans. J. Cunningham (Dublin, 1958, with many reprints), 186.

[12]Charlesworth, J., *The Messiah*, 5.

[13]Charlesworth, J., *The Messiah*, 4.

Jews did not have a unified vision of a Messiah.[14]

Contradictorily, the conservative Charlesworth also argues that there is some evidence that before Mark, there was an idea of a Christian-type Messiah among Jews, but he is wrong. He concedes that the death of the Messiah in 4 Ezra is not efficacious,[15] which contradicts the Christian idea that Christ's sacrifice saved humanity from its sins. He rejects the rabbinic evidence of a dying Messiah as too late (post 2nd cent. CE). He also stipulates that there is no reference to a Davidic Messiah in the pre-70 CE period[16] and informs us that scholars agree that "*the* Messiah" is not referred to in the *Jewish Scriptures*. But Charlesworth accepts the dying Messiah of 4 Ezra 7.29 even though he admits that 4 Ezra was edited by the church!

The term *messiah* rarely appears in any Jewish literature written between 250 BCE and 200 CE. The Mishnah (ca 200 CE), Philo, and Josephus omit any mention of a coming Messiah, as do the thirteen books of the Apocrypha. Most of the passages referring to *messiah* are found in the Pseudepigrapha (52 documents) and in the Dead Sea Scrolls.[17] Here are some of Charlesworth's conclusions about three of the four documents that he believes were put in their final state between 50 BCE and 100 CE which contain the term *Messiah* or *Christ*.[18] Is the Messiah portrayed as a king? One verse in Psalms of Solomon is ambiguous. God is the chief figure, not the Messiah. In 4 Ezra and in 2 Baruch, though the Messiah is present, he has no functions. Does the Messiah resurrect the dead? Only in 4 Ezra 7.28-29, a Christian interpolation. Is the Messiah human rather than divine? Yes. The Pseudepigrapha illustrate that the concept of messianism was not universal, uniform, or Christian-like by the first century CE.

Turning to the Dead Sea Scrolls, Charlesworth writes that of the more than 170 documents "created, written, or redacted at Qumran" only three referred to a messiah: the Rule of the Community (1QS), the Rule of the Congregation (1QSa), and

---

[14]Ibid.

[15]Charlesworth, J., *The Messiah*, 8.

[16]Charlesworth, J., *The Messiah*, 8-9.

[17]Charlesworth, J., *The Messiah*, 11-12,16.

[18]Charlesworth, J., *The Messiah*, 20-24.

the Damascus Document (CD).[19] The messiah of the Dead Sea Scrolls bears little resemblance to the Messiah of the gospels.

Charlesworth rightly asserts that, "The gospels and Paul must not be read as if they were reliable sources for pre-70 Jewish beliefs in the Messiah."[20] We conclude that the Christian Messiah is a creation of the early church and does not derive from Judaism.

Son of Man: Daniel Chapter 7

The *son of man* passages in the gospels derive from Daniel 7. In a vision, Daniel sees four animals in succession. Then "one that is 'ancient of days' takes his seat on a throne of fiery flames...." At the end of the dream, Daniel writes:

> I was looking in a night vision and, behold, one like a son of man was coming with the clouds of heaven and went as far as the Ancient of Days and was brought near him. Sovereignty, glory and kingship were given him, and all the peoples, nations and languages were to serve him. His sovereignty was to be an eternal sovereignty never to cease and his kingship imperishable. (Daniel 7.13,14[21])

The *Parables of Enoch* (1 Enoch 37-71) suspiciously contains the only reference to *son of man* as a title in pre-70 CE Jewish literature, but it is found 14 times in the gospel of Mark where Jesus, and only he, applies the title to himself.

Geza Vermes dates the *Parables* to the last quarter of the first century CE.[22] In *Jesus the Jew*, he asserts that the phrase *son of man* is used as a substitute for the personal pronoun "I."[23] It is normally used this way in the *Jewish Scriptures* and in rabbinic literature. Vermes writes, "...no trace survives of its titular use, from which it must be inferred that there is no case to be made

[19]Charlesworth, J., *The Messiah*, 24,25.

[20]Charlesworth, J., *The Messiah*, 35.

[21]as quoted by Geza Vermes, *Jesus the Jew*, 169

[22]Vermes, Geza, *Jesus the Jew*, 160-191.

[23]Vermes, Geza, *Jesus the Jew*, 163.

for an eschatological or messianic officeholder generally known as 'the "son of man"''" prior to Mark in 70 CE.[24]

Dan 7.9-14 was seen by second-century exegetes as depicting an *exalted* David or Messiah, not a suffering and dying one[25] which would be incompatible with the triumphal image of the *son of man* in Daniel 7.[26] H. Conzelman asserts that "...all the 'son of man' utterances [are] foreign to Jesus."[27] In addition, the Jewish literature written before 200 CE contains no evidence of a Messiah whose death is efficacious, nor one to whom divine functions are attributed, such as judging the dead, forgiving sins, etc., and, of course, we do not find a Messiah who is depicted as divine or the Son of God. We agree with Vermes and H. Conzelman that the messianic exegesis of Dan 7.13 does not go back to Jesus.[28] Where does *son of man* as a messianic title come from? Vermes concludes his chapter in *Jesus the Jew* on the *son of man* with a quote from Paul Winter. Reviewing Norman Perrin's *Rediscovering the Teaching of Jesus*, P. Winter writes, "If Perrin's interpretation of the 'son of man' sayings in the Synoptic Gospels is correct — and it is supported by Vermes's... study of the linguistic use of 'bar-nash(a)' in Jewish Aramaic — then the place of origin of the myth [of the 'son of man'] is not to be sought in Iran, or in Judea or even in Ugarit, but in the German universities."[29]

Jesus' 1st Prediction of his Death: Mk 8.31-33

Immediately after Peter's declaration, Jesus makes the first of three predictions concerning his own suffering, death, and resurrection. In private he instructs the disciples that the son of man must suffer greatly, "and be rejected by the elders, the chief priests, and the scribes, and be killed, and after three days rise again" (Mk 8.31). (Matthew names the place of Jesus' death as Jerusalem; Mark does not.) Taking Jesus aside, Peter strongly

---

[24]Ibid.

[25]Vermes, Geza, *Jesus the Jew*, 175.

[26]ibid.

[27]Vermes, Geza, *Jesus the Jew*, 177.

[28]Vermes, Geza, *Jesus the Jew*, 186.

[29]Ibid., n 91, p 261. P. Winter, Deutsche Literaturzeitung 89 (1968), col. 784.

condemns him for this prophecy. In response Jesus curses Peter saying, "Get behind me, Satan!" (Mk 8.33). He denounces Peter for thinking of human rather than divine things. Matthew continues to rehabilitate Peter. His Peter, referring to Jesus' death, says only, "God forbid it, Lord! This must never happen to you" (Mt 16.22). Luke goes further than Matthew, and drops all reference to Peter's rebuking of Jesus. The other disciples make no response to any of this.

The detailed nature of the three predictions of Jesus' death has caused most scholars to conclude that these prophecies come from Mark or the early Marcan community, not from Jesus. Originally Jesus was not aware of his upcoming death.

Jesus tells the disciples and the crowd to take up the cross and follow him (Mk 8.34,38). Again, the church indicates that Jesus knows of his death and voluntarily submits to it. But how did Jesus know that the method of execution would be crucifixion as this was a Roman, not a Jewish method of execution?

Certain people from India tell Alexander the Great that he "must die at the hands of [his] own people."[30] Plutarch says that Heracles, the son of Zeus, suffered painfully in performing his labors.[31] Jesus is virtuous like Alexander and suffers like Heracles. The HCNT editors think that these traditions perhaps were familiar to the early Christians.[32]

The custom of giving divine titles like *Son of God* to rulers was common in Egypt and the East. The Rosetta Stone proclaimed the Greek king of Egypt, Ptolemy V Epiphanes (210-180 BCE), to be divine; he is described as "...restorer of the life of man... child of the Gods through the love of the Father... *living image of Zeus*, Son of the Sun... priest of [the divine] Alexander and the Savior Gods and the Benefactor Gods and the Gods of the love of the Father, the God visible, for whom thanks be given."[33] Jesus is called *Son of God* thirty-nine times in the *Christian Scriptures*. When "the high priest [asks Jesus], 'Are you the Messiah, the Son of the Blessed One?' Jesus says, 'I am;...'" (Mk 14.61-62).

The pagan Celsus complains that if Christians believe in the miracles of Jesus, such as his miraculous birth, and if they

---

[30]Boring, M., HCNT, 105, #121 Pseudo-Callisthenes.

[31]Boring, M., HCNT, 106, #122.

[32]Ibid.

[33]Cartlidge, D., 14.

accept that Jesus was raised from the dead and ascended to heaven, "then how can [they] refuse to believe precisely the same stories when they are told of other Savior Gods: Herakles, Asklepios, the Dioscuri, Dionysos, and a dozen others I could name?"[34] For more on the Savior Gods, see Chapter 9.

Cartlidge and Dungan point out that for the ancients there were two kinds of savior gods. First, there are gods like Hercules who have divine and human parents and perform great deeds that benefit humankind "and so... were rewarded with immortality, and worshiped as Saviors." The second type of savior god is identified with "great leaders, especially kings, [who are] in fact temporary manifestations or appearances (*epiphaneia*) of the eternal Gods themselves"[35] (Cartlidge's ital.), for example, Julius Caesar and Augustus. The Egyptian king has a special relationship with the Father. Plutarch points out that many eastern kings were given the title, god, or son of a god (cf. Mk 8.27-30).[36] Also, the editors of HCNT point out that the suffering of the Son of God, "was not a completely unfamiliar tradition" to the Christians.[37]

Transfiguration of Jesus: Mk 9.2-10

Six days after the first prophecy of his death, Jesus takes Peter, James, and John to a high mountain (Mk 9.2) where he is transfigured, his clothes become a dazzling white (9.3). Homer writes that "from the divine body of the goddess a light shone... so that the strong house was filled with brightness as of lightening...."[38] The editors of HCNT conclude that "light on the face or the whole body points as such to one's nature as son of God...."[39]

Elijah and Moses appear and talk with Jesus, (about what we do not know). A voice comes from a cloud, announcing that this is "my Son, the Beloved; listen to him!" (Mk 9.7). The Jewish

---

[34]Cartlidge, D., 17, quoting from Origen's *Against Celsus.*

[35]Cartlidge, D., 18.

[36]Boring, M., HCNT, 104, #120, Plutarch Moralia, "On Inoffensive Self-Praise" 12.

[37]Boring, M., HCNT, 106, #122, Plutarch Moralia, "On the Fortune or the Virtue of Alexander" 11.

[38]Boring, M., HCNT, 107, #125, From the Homeric Hymns 2,275-80.

[39]Boring, M., HCNT, 108, #126.

prophets suddenly disappear in a cloud; only Jesus remains. Jesus replaces Moses (the Jewish law) and Elijah (the prophets).

Matthew continues to elevate the status of Jesus. The disciples fall on their faces before the divine Jesus. Luke at last reveals what Jesus has been talking about with the prophets, his departure "which he was about to accomplish at Jerusalem" (Lk 9.31).

Coming down the mountain, Jesus commands the disciples to be silent "about what they had seen, until after the Son of Man had risen from the dead" (Mk 9.9). Mark sticks with his depiction of the disciples as spiritually blind; they wonder what the "rising from the dead" might mean. But Jews had known about the concept of resurrection at least since ca 165 BCE when the book of Daniel was written. Matthew, elevating Jesus again, drops the wondering. Luke, growing uncomfortable with the messianic secret, merely states that the disciples told no one what they had seen (Lk 9.36).

The Last Exorcism

After the transfiguration, there is a final exorcism. This cure brackets Jesus' public ministry; he begins with an exorcism of a Jewish man in the synagogue, and ends with an exorcism of a pagan, another foreshadowing of the church's mission to non-Jews. Effectively, the ministry ended before Peter's declaration. Why was this exorcism added to Mark's text? Probably because in Matthew, Luke and John there is a tendency to elongate Jesus' ministry right up to the time of his arrest. For example, in Matthew he cures people in the temple in Jerusalem (21.14).

After Jesus and his three disciples come down from the mountain, a father complains that Jesus' disciples could not cast out an unclean spirit from his son. Jesus exorcises the spirit and says to his disciples that this kind requires prayer (Mk 8.29), though Jesus has not prayed, and one would have thought that he would already have taught his disciples to pray.

The pagan philosopher, Empedocles, had power over evil spirits, too. He led the soul of a dead man from Hades.[40] In this Marcan exorcism story, the father asks that Jesus help his unbelief

---

[40]Martin, F., 175-76.

(Mk 9.24) which is paralleled in a pagan inscription in which a woman named Ambrosia is healed of her blindness and unbelief.[41]

Second Prediction of Jesus' Death

Jesus is passing through Galilee. He makes a second prediction of his death, again privately to the disciples who still do not understand why he must die, but are too fearful to ask him about it (Mk 9.31-32). Matthew substitutes "distressed" for "fearful" and drops the reference to the disciples' lack of understanding. Amazingly, Luke writes that the meaning of Jesus' passion "was concealed from them, so that they could not perceive it" (Lk 9.45). God is concealing the kingdom from Jesus' disciples!

Jesus leaves pagan territory and returns to Capernaum in Galilee. In "the house" Jesus asks the twelve what they had argued about on the way to Capernaum. They inform him that they were disputing as to who was the greatest among them (Mk 9.33). Were they fighting over political power?

The disciple, John, says to Jesus that a non-follower of Jesus was using his name to cast out demons (Mk 9.38). The disciples inform Jesus that they had tried to stop the exorcist, but Jesus says, "Whoever is not against us is for us" (9.40). Luke agrees, but Matthew has the opposite, "Whoever is not with me is against me...." (Mt 12.30).

Mark states that Jesus teaches, "it is better for you to enter the kingdom of God with one eye than to have two eyes and be thrown into hell [Gehenna], where the worm never dies, and the fire is never quenched" (Mk 9.47-48; cf. Isa 66.24). Plato says, "Men are prepared to have their own feet and hands cut off if they feel these... to be harmful"[42] to their virtue.

On Divorce: Mk 10.2-12

Jesus leaves "that place" for "the region of Judea and beyond the Jordan" (Mk 10.1). He teaches the crowds, "as was his custom," but does he do so in parables?

---

[41]Martin, F., 226.
[42]Boring, M., HCNT, 113, #136.

Some Pharisees, wanting to trap Jesus, asked him, "Is it lawful for a man to divorce his wife?" Jesus asked them what Moses had said, and they answer that Moses' commandment allowed a man to divorce his wife by writing a certificate of dismissal and giving it to her. Jesus responds, "Because of your hardness of heart [Moses] wrote this commandment..." (Mk 10.2-5), and Jesus forbids all divorce (Mk 10.9). Note that it was not Moses who allowed divorce, for the Commandments are from God.

When Jesus is alone in "the house" with his disciples, he explains that if a husband or wife divorces his or her mate and marries another, she or he commits adultery (Mk 10.12); however a Jewish woman could not initiate a divorce (cf. Dt 24.1). In a Jewish certificate of divorce from Masada (ca 111 CE), a man initiates a divorce and both are allowed to remarry.[43] Also, under Roman law, a husband or wife could initiate a divorce and both are free to remarry.[44] Against Mark, Matthew's Jesus allows divorce if *pornai* is involved, i.e., an impropriety which would include adultery, but is not limited to it (Mt 19.9). The Pythagoreans also forbade divorce.[45]

The Rich Man

A rich man asks Jesus what he must do to "inherit eternal life" (Mk 10.17; Mt 19.29). Jesus lists five of the Ten Commandments: the prohibition against murder, adultery, theft, bearing false witness, and dishonoring one's father or mother (Mk 10.19). He adds a commandment of his own, i.e., not to defraud people. Matthew and Luke correct this by omitting it (Mt 19.18; Lk 18.20). Note that Jesus omits the specifically Jewish commandments: the acceptance of only one God, the prohibition against graven images (idols), keeping the Sabbath, the prohibition against the misuse of God's name.

The rich man says that he has observed these moral laws since his youth. Jesus tells him to go and "sell what you own and give the money to the poor" (Mk 10.21). The Marcan Jesus and his disciples never give money to the poor, and this is the

---

[43]Boring, M., HCNT, 58, #35.
[44]Boring, M., HCNT, 117, #142.
[45]Boring, M., HCNT, 117, #142.

only place where Jesus advises anyone to do so. The man goes away grieving, not wanting to part with his wealth.

Jesus tells the disciples how hard it is for the rich to enter the kingdom of God, "It is easier for a camel to go through the eye of a needle than for" the rich "to enter the kingdom of God" (Mk 10.25). Despite the modern image of Jesus favoring the poor over the rich, there are a number of pro-rich stories in Matthew and Luke (see Mt 25.14-28; Lk 19.11-27; Lk 16.10-13). The church gradually attracted rich, as well as poor, people and thus the presence of both pro rich and anti-rich sayings.

Pagans, too, taught the worthlessness of wealth and flesh compared to the soul. The Pythagoreans taught, "When the body is left behind you will achieve eternal liberty, you will be an immortal and incorruptible God, no longer a mortal being."[46] For the Stoics, the soul is a divine spark, "a fragment of God..."[47] Seneca writes, "*God is near you, he is with you, he is within you... a holy spirit indwells within us, one who marks our good and bad deeds...*"[48] (Reale's ital.). Seneca believes that "the untamed spirit" waits "only to be released from the body before it soars to highest heaven."[49] The soul is burdened by the flesh, the mind is free and "candid to the Gods...." "This poor body [is] the prison and fetter of the soul." And the Pythagoreans teach, "When the body is left behind you will achieve eternal liberty, you will be an immortal and incorruptible god, no longer a mortal being."[50] Epictetus holds a similar attitude, "But the body is nothing to me: the parts of it are nothing to me. Death? Let it come when it chooses...."[51]

With reference to entering the kingdom, Mark says that all things are possible with God (Mk 10.27; Mt 19.26; Lk 18.27). The pagan magical papyri state that, "All things are possible to this god."[52]

To the rewards one will get in this life, Jesus adds "persecu-

---

[46]Reale, G., 261

[47]Reale, G., 84, quoting Epictetus.

[48]Reale, G., 59, quoting Seneca's 41st letter.

[49]Reale, G., 61, and following two quotes.

[50]Reale, G. 261.

[51]Epictetus, *Discourses of Epictetus, The: The Handbook, Fragments*, Robin Hard, Translator (London: Orion Publishing Group, 1995), Bk 3.22.

[52]Smith, M., *Magician*, 205, PGM XIII.713.

tions" (Mk 10.30). Apparently the early church felt oppressed. This is another passage created by the early church to provide moral support for the ostracized Christians. Suffering in and of itself is a positive good in Christian thought, but not in Jewish thought.

Third Prediction of Jesus' Death

At last, Mark tells us where Jesus is heading, namely to Jerusalem (Mk 10.32). Jesus takes the twelve aside and predicts his death for the third and last time, "the Son of Man will be handed over to the chief priests and scribes, and they will condemn him to death...." This is the first time that Jesus adds that "the Gentiles" will mock, spit, scourge, and kill him. He also adds that after three days he will rise again. As to the suffering, again Mark is using the *Jewish Scriptures* to construct Jesus' biography. Compare Isa 53.10, "Yet it was the will of the LORD to crush him with pain... his life [is] an offering for sin..." Luke adds that "everything that is written about the Son of Man by the prophets will be accomplished" (Lk 18.31). Luke again says that the twelve did not understand his prediction because its meaning "was hidden from them" (Lk 18.34). God is still concealing the plan from Jesus' own disciples.

Mark reveals (Mk 10.35-45) that the disciples still have no faith; they are expecting an earthly kingdom. James and John ask that they be allowed to sit on the right and left hand of Jesus when he comes in power. Hercules and Asclepius also fight over who should be ranked above the other.[53] Jesus asks if they are able to "drink his cup" and "accept his baptism." They say they are. Jesus then predicts that they will be martyred (Mk 10.39), an early church tradition.

Jesus preaches that he has come "to give his life [as] a ransom for many" (Mk 10.45). But to whom will God pay the ransom? To Satan, who is holding humanity captive. This view was not abandoned by the church for more than a thousand years.

At some point Jesus arrives at Jericho (Mk 10.46-52) about ten miles from Jerusalem; he then leaves Jericho. (Not a lot of activity in this city.) As Jesus leaves Jericho, he cures a blind

---

[53]Cotter, W., Miracles, 27, #1.30.

beggar who addresses him as "Son of David." This is a royal messianic title, a hint that Jesus is a political Messiah, a king. After the man is cured, he follows Jesus (Mk 10.46-48,52).

Chapter 6

Jerusalem

Brown and Fitzmyer simply do not want to accept the fact that Jesus has deceived the Jewish crowds and that they perceive him as a king.
— Authors

And the foreigners who join themselves to the LORD,.... these I will bring to my holy mountain, and make them joyful in my house of prayer; their burnt offerings and their sacrifices will be accepted on my altar; for my house shall be called a house of prayer for all peoples.
— Isaiah 56.6-7

My house... you have made it a den of robbers...
— Mark 11.17

Mark relates that Jesus left "that place," heading for "the region of Judea beyond the Jordan" (Mk 10.1; Mt 19.1-2). Luke dramatically announces that Jesus "set his face to go to Jerusalem" (Lk 9.51), again emphasizing Jesus' deliberate intent to carry out the plan of God in Jerusalem.

Royal Reception: Mk 11.1-10

Jesus, his disciples, and a large crowd travel from Jericho, about ten miles east of Jerusalem, to Bethphage and Bethany, which are near the Mount of Olives, a stone's throw from the Eastern Gate of Jerusalem in Judea. Actually Bethany would have come first, since Jesus was traveling from east to west (Matthew drops Bethany, 21.1). Jesus orders two (unnamed) disciples to

89

go ahead to (an unnamed) village near the Mount of Olives, and says that they "...will find tied there a colt that has never been ridden; untie it and bring it..." (Mk 11.2). Jesus says that if the owner asks why the two disciples need the donkey, they are to say, "The Lord needs it and will send it back here immediately" (Mk 11.3). Note that Jesus refers to himself as *Lord* (*kyrios*), a title commonly used as a reference to God in the *Jewish Scriptures*, and also one that is used in the pagan mystery religions. The two disciples bring the donkey to Jesus.

Jesus mounts the colt and rides toward the Eastern Gate of Jerusalem. Many people spread their cloaks, as well as leafy branches, on the road in front of the colt Jesus is riding (Mk 11.8). Matthew again says explicitly that Jesus is fulfilling ancient prophecies from the Jewish Scriptures. "Look, your king is coming to you, humble and mounted on a donkey, and on a colt, the foal of a donkey" (Mt 21.4-5; Zch 9.9). Matthew has misunderstood Hebrew parallelism and thinks the prophet is referring to two animals and has Jesus sit on both (Mt 21.7)! Scholars identify the prophet as Zechariah, even though Zch 9.9 was not applied to the Messiah until well after the time of Jesus.

Luke, against Mark and Matthew, says the crowd is composed of "the whole multitude" of Jesus' disciples (Lk 19.37-38), apparently thousands from Galilee (Lk 12.1). Many people welcome Jesus, shouting, "Hosanna! Blessed is the one who comes in the name of the Lord! Blessed is the coming kingdom of our ancestor David! Hosanna in the highest heaven!" (Mk 11.9-10; cf. 2 Sam 14.4; 2 Kgs 6.26). This is a variant quote of the royal Psalm (118.25-29; cf. 2 Sam 7.16) used in blessing the king at his coronation.

Only Luke has some Pharisees in the crowd warn Jesus to order his disciples to stop accepting this royal welcome (Lk 19.39). Luke realized that a powerful Roman official like the prefect Pilate, would recognize that the acceptance of royal honors was a treasonous act under Roman law, one punishable by death. Needing to fulfill the divine plan, Jesus rejects the advice of the Pharisees, saying, "I tell you, if these were silent, the stones would shout out" (Lk 19.40).

J. Fitzmyer asserts that Luke is telling us that "the Jews"

have misunderstood Jesus' ministry.[1] Misunderstood? Jesus has preached about the kingdom of God during his ministry. He is perceived by his own disciples as a royal claimant. At Jericho Jesus accepts the royal title Son of David from the blind man and here, approaching the capital of Judea, Jesus purposefully rides a colt in fulfillment of a royal Psalm (118.26), and accepts the shouts of the crowd acknowledging his kingship. All of this makes it clear that Jesus intends to convey the idea that he is a king, one who is about to come into his power.

R. Brown, like Fitzmyer, argues that the Jewish crowd misunderstands Jesus' mission and expects a nationalist hero.[2] According to Brown, the crowd should have understood Jesus as what? A peaceful, humble, and non-treasonous Messiah since Zch 9.9 talks of a peaceful and humble king! We would agree, if the crowds were composed of scholarly Christian exegetes like Raymond Brown and Joseph Fitzmyer.

R. Brown concedes that a "triumph" was "the normal Greek expression used to describe joyful reception of Hellenistic sovereigns into the city."[3] Titus was greeted this way at Antioch and when Cato retired from the military, his soldiers threw "their mantles down for him to walk upon."[4] But Brown still sticks to his guns — the crowds were expecting what, a spiritual Messiah?

Brown and Fitzmyer simply do not want to accept the fact that Jesus has deceived the Jewish crowds who thus perceive him as a king.

Riot in the Temple: Mk 11.11,15-19

At Mark 11.11, Jesus enters Jerusalem and immediately goes to the temple. He looks around but since it is late in the day he leaves, traveling with the twelve to Bethany.

The next day on the way back to Jerusalem, Jesus is hungry but finds no figs on a tree by the roadside, since it is not the right season. He curses it, "May no one ever eat fruit from you again" (Mk 11.14). The following day, after the temple riot, Jesus

---

[1] Fitzmyer, J., *Luke*, vol 2, 1241-1252.

[2] Brown, Raymond, *The Gospel According to John*, 2 vols., 1966 (The Anchor Bible. Garden City: Doubleday & Company, Inc., 1986), vol 1, 462.

[3] Brown, R., *John*, vol 1, 462.

[4] Boring, M., HCNT, Plutarch, 123, #156.

and the disciples again travel to Jerusalem and the disciples see
that the tree is withered (Mk 11.21-22). The fig tree is Judaism.
Jesus is teaching that a truly divine religion would never be out
of season; it would always provide spiritual sustenance for its
believers. Judaism is to be replaced by Christianity.

Between the cursing of the fig tree and its withering, Jesus
returns to the temple and violently drives out those who buy and
sell the animals intended for sacrifice; he overturns the tables of
the money-changers, and the seats of those who sell doves. No
Jewish Messiah would riot against people for performing tasks
necessary for worship in the temple. Animals are needed for
sacrifice and, if all those pagan coins describing the emperor as
"Son of God" and "Savior of the World" are to be kept out of the
temple, money changers are needed to exchange the pagan coins
for Jewish ones.

Jesus preaches, "My house... you have made it a den of robbers" (Mk 11.17; cf. Jer 7.11; Isa 56.7). The Synoptic Jesus
thinks that selling animals for sacrifice is thievery. John omits
the reference to robbers, but still sees business in the temple as
wrong. At least John has changed Jesus' phrase "my house" to
"my father's house," recognizing that it would be blasphemous
for Jesus to refer to God's temple as "my house."

For Luke the story of the temple riot involves much too much
violence on the part of the Prince of Peace. Fitzmyer[5] notes that
Luke has removed all details of violence from the story. Well,
most of it — Jesus still "drives out" those who are selling things
(Lk 19.45). Luke adds that "the chief priests, the scribes and
the leaders of the people kept looking for a way to kill him" (Lk
19.47).

Origen (ca 240 CE), the best Christian exegete of the third
century, pointed out that Jesus would have been arrested immediately, which is why he rejects the scene as unhistorical.
Fitzmyer agrees that Jesus' attack on the temple "would have
provoked an immediate reaction from the priests and officials in
the Temple,"[6] as rioting was a death penalty offense under Roman law and a criminal act under Jewish law. Fitzmyer counters
that Jesus was put on trial "quickly." But the temple police and

---

[5]Fitzmyer, J., *Luke*, vol 2, 1261.
[6]Fitzmyer, J., *Luke*, vol 2, 1264.

Roman authorities would hardly have waited several days to arrest the law breaker. And John, placing the riot at the beginning of Jesus' three-year ministry, rather than arresting Jesus immediately, has "the Jews" blandly inquire, "What sign can you show us, authorizing you to do these things?" (Jn 2.18).

Let us examine some additional problems connected with the temple riot. Jesus prophesies, "My house shall be called a house of prayer for all nations" (Mk 11.17; Isa 56.7). Matthew and Luke, thinking that the temple was destroyed before Jesus' prophecy could be fulfilled, omit the prophecy. But non-Jews were already praying at the temple in the time of Jesus (see Josephus and Philo). Mark relates that the riot occurred on the day after Jesus entered Jerusalem. Conversely, Matthew and Luke depict the riot as occurring on the day that Jesus enters Jerusalem. And John places it at the beginning of Jesus' ministry, some years earlier (Jn 2.13-17).

Jesus invalidates the temple by his actions, but no Jewish prophet or Messiah would dream of abolishing a fundamental institution of Judaism. The temple is mentioned over 900 times in the *Jewish Scriptures*. Many modern Christian apologists argue that there was a strong Jewish anti-temple movement in first-century Judaism. Yet in Mark, Jesus praises the widow's contribution to the temple treasury (Mk 12.42-44), and he pays the temple tax for Peter and himself, granted without great enthusiasm (at Mt 17.24ff). There is no mention of an anti-temple faction in the works of either Philo of Alexandria or Josephus. In the Dead Sea Scrolls, the Qumranites opposed the priestly administration of the temple in Jerusalem, but not the sacred temple itself.

Some Teachings in the Temple: Mark 12.13-44

We will discuss the story of the "wicked tenants" (Mk 12.112) in Chapter 7.

"They" send some Pharisees and Herodians to the temple to trap Jesus by asking him if it is lawful to pay taxes to Caesar, knowing that to withhold taxes was treason under Roman law. Jesus replies that one should render to God the things that are God's and to the emperor what is his (Mk 12.13-14; cf. Acts 5.37). Josephus condemned Judas the Galilean in 6 CE because the rebel refused to pay Roman taxes (Mk 12.13-17; cf. Acts 5.37).[7] Jesus is careful to command his followers to obey secular law. Thus the theory that Jesus is a freedom fighter (held by H. Maccoby, S.G.F. Brandon and others) who opposes Roman tyranny is not feasible.

Jesus is asked by a scribe what is the most important commandment (Mk 12.31-33). Jesus quotes part of the Shema, an important Jewish prayer. In part it states that one should love God and love one's neighbor (Mk 12.28-29). The scribe responds, "This is much more important than all whole burnt offerings and sacrifices" (Mk 12.33); compare Amos 5.21-24 which relates that the Lord says he hates festivals and sacrifice, preferring justice and righteousness (cf. Ps 40.6-8; 1 Sam 15.22). However, Amos is referring to a balance between ethical and ritual law, not to a rejection of sacrifice, etc. Mark tells us, "After that, no one dared to ask [Jesus] a question" (vs. 34)! Another non-dialogue.

We will not dwell on the convoluted argument at Mk 12.35-37 which says that Jesus can't be David's son, because in the *Jewish Scriptures* he is called David's Lord (cf. Ps 110.1). We would merely note that Mark, or his editor, does not always want to associate Jesus with the Jewish Messiah.

Jewish Law

In the temple, a large crowd listens to Jesus "with delight" (Mk 12.37b). Jesus says to beware of the scribes; they wear long robes and want respect in the market places, and to have "the best seats in the synagogues and places of honor at banquets!" (Mk 12.38-39). Jesus preaches that the scribes "devour widows' houses, and for the sake of appearance say long prayers" (Mk 12.40). He says, "They will receive the greater condemnation." A Jewish audience would hardly be happy with a Jewish teacher who slanders and condemns their religious leaders.

Matthew and Luke greatly expand the anti-Jewish material of Mk 12.38-40. In Matthew Jesus lacerates the religious leaders while in the temple. He says the scribes and Pharisees are hypocrites and "are as graves" and whitewashed tombs (Mt 23.27). Jesus preaches that the scribes and Pharisees are hypocrites,

---

[7]Boring, M., HCNT, 126, #160.

"For you lock people out of the kingdom of Heaven..." S. Lachs states that rabbinic tradition held that hypocrites, liars, etc., could not "...receive the face of the Shekinah,"[8] i.e., God would not receive them. Jesus adds that they "make the new convert twice as much a child of hell [Gehenna] as [themselves]" (Mt 23.13,15), but the Pharisees had no authority outside of Judea.

Matthew and Luke provide scriptural support for the widely-held but erroneous Christian belief that Jews consider the law to be a burden which they groaned under. The scribes and Pharisees, Jesus says, load people with heavy burdens hard to bear, and do not "lift a finger" to ease them (Mt 23.4; Lk 11.46). It is true that obeying all the 613 commandments is more demanding than keeping the few ethical commandments required of non-Jews. However, for Jews, observing God's law is a privilege. The Psalmist writes, "The law of the Lord is perfect, reviving the soul.... the precepts of the Lord are right, rejoicing the heart..." (Ps 19.7). "I delight in the way of your decrees... I will delight in your statutes; ..." (Ps 119.14,16). There are many more such passages throughout the *Jewish Scriptures* (cf. Ps 40.8; Prv 29.18, etc.), as well as in the rabbinical writings.

The Lukan Jesus is heading for Jerusalem but, while still in Galilee, he and others are invited by a Pharisee to dine in his home (Lk 11.37). The host is amazed that Jesus has not ritually washed his hands before dinner (Lk 11.38). One has to marvel at the audacity of the Lukan Jesus; reading his host's mind, Jesus launches into a long, ill-tempered diatribe against his host and the other guests. What has happened to the traditional hospitality of the Near East, the courtesy paid to the host by the guest?

Jesus says they (the Pharisees) are "full of greed and wickedness," and condemns them for giving alms instead of giving of themselves, for tithing "everything" and neglecting "justice and mercy and faith" (Lk 11.39-42; Mt 23.23). No Jewish teacher would think of tithing as a trivial commandment, as compared to faith, justice, and the love of God, for all are considered sacred, coming from God.[9]

---

[8]Lachs, S. *Commentary*, 368, n 32, B. Sot. 41b, B. Yom, 86b.

[9]For extensive information concerning first-century Judaism, see the works of E.P. Sanders, especially *Paul and Palestinian Judaism, Jewish Law from Jesus to the Mishnah* and *Judaism: Practice and Belief 63 BCE-66 CE*.

The Lukan Jesus states that "their" Jewish ancestors killed the prophets (cf. Mt 23.30-31). He continues to denounce the lawyers, "You build the tombs of the prophets whom your ancestors killed" (Lk 11.47; Mt 23.29). Jesus charges that Jews have killed all the prophets "since the foundation of the world," from Abel to Zechariah (Lk 11.50-51). Of course, the *Jewish Scriptures* do not indicate that the Jewish people have "killed all the prophets" from Genesis to 2 Chronicles. Luke and Matthew simply want to condemn Jewish leaders and the Jewish people as faithless murderers.

Jesus adds "I will send [to Jews] prophets and apostles, some of whom they will kill and persecute" (Lk 11.49). Matthew's Jesus says, "some... you will kill and crucify, and some you will flog in your synagogues and pursue from town to town" (Mt 23.34-35; cf. Mk 13.9). nowhere in Acts of the Apostles, Paul's letters, or later Christian history is there a record of Jews crucifying Christians. As to Mark 13.9, there is no organized persecution of Christians by Jews until Acts, written long after Mark's gospel.

There is still more — the lawyers take away "the key of knowledge;..." (Lk 11.52), i.e., Jews misunderstand the *Jewish Scriptures*, that is, they don't have Jesus' Christian understanding of the Scriptures. Finally, the Lukan diatribe ends, and Jesus leaves the Pharisee's home. The scribes and the Pharisees lie "in wait for him, to catch him in something he might say" (Lk 11.54). (Haven't they heard enough already?)

Compare the list of slanders aimed at the Pharisees in Mk 12.37-40 and Mt 23.1-31 with this pagan list of insults.[10] Dio Cocceianus (1st cent. CE) gives this list of his opponents' vices: he calls them sophists, ignorant, boastful, unlearned, evil spirited, impious, liars. He also says that his opponents teach for money and that they are mindless and shameless and deceive others and themselves.[11]

Many writers view Jesus as a Jewish reformer. This is surely not based on the rage of these passages. Could Jewish soil have produced such fundamental anti-Jewishness?

Jesus praises a widow who gives her food money to the temple treasury (Mk 12.41-44). Euripides (485-406 BCE) writes that

---

[10]Boring, M., HCNT, 132, #169.
[11]Boring, M., HCNT, 132, #169.

those who are poor and give small gifts to the gods have more piety than "those that bring oxen to sacrifice."[12]

Apocalypse: Mark 13

Arriving at the temple, Jesus and his disciples marvel at the largeness of the temple stones and buildings. Was this their first visit? One assumes that Jesus and his disciples had in the past traveled to Jerusalem for the festivals. Luke states that "some" spoke of the temple as "adorned with noble stones and offerings" (Lk 21.5). Luke cannot imply that Jesus has never seen the temple complex before, since in Luke's birth narrative he maintains that Jesus' parents came to the temple every year for Passover (Lk 2.41). John omits the whole incident.

In Mark, on the Mount of Olives near Jerusalem, Jesus speaks privately to four of his disciples, coldly predicting the destruction of the temple. "Do you see these great buildings? Not one stone will be left here upon another; all will be thrown down" (Mk 13.2). The temple is a central institution of Judaism, yet Jesus' disciples respond only by blandly inquiring as to when this destruction will occur and what are the signs of the end (Mk 13.4).[13] Jesus teaches that wars and rumors of war, earthquakes and famines, will proceed the destruction (Mk 13.8), but in what time period do these not occur?

The prophecy of the destruction of Jerusalem and the world is judgmental in Mark. This passage (Mk 13.9-13) has been interpreted by some writers as pointing to the destruction of Jerusalem by Rome, and by others as predicting a distant cosmic apocalypse. Many argue that Jesus predicted an imminent end of the world.

In Mark, Jesus preaches that "there are some standing here who will not taste death until they see that the kingdom of God has come with power" (Mk 9.1), indicating Jesus is expecting that the end of the world will be soon. Luke emphasizes that salvation is accomplished now, in the present (realized eschatology), and John nearly obliterates the idea of future salvation in favor of the view that salvation has already occurred.

---

[12]Boring, M., HCNT, 178, #244.
[13]Boring, M., HCNT, 135, 136, 137, 142, 82.

Josephus[14] relates how the leading Jewish citizens and the Roman procurator, Albinus, reacted to predictions of doom. A farmer named Jesus predicts the coming destruction of the temple, Jerusalem, and its inhabitants. After several years of these prophecies, the farmer is chastised by the leading citizens and turned over to Albinus who scourges him and, thinking him crazy, releases him. The farmer later dies during the first war with Rome. Is this not a bit of evidence that possibly the evangelists may have used the writings of Josephus in composing their gospels?

Greco-Romans, too, knew about an apocalypse. Compare Revelation 8 & 9 with the Stoic Seneca's (ca 3 CE-ca 65 CE) description of the end of the world in his letter to Marcia. In Revelation, the angels of destruction destroy one-third of all trees and all green grass, and a third of the sea becomes blood. The bottomless pit is opened (Rev 9.1ff). "They were allowed to torture [those without seals] for five months but not to kill them" (Rev 9.5). An army of 200,000 destroys people, one-third are killed by fire, smoke, and brimstone, "...if they did not repent, worshiping devils and idols of gold and silver and stone and wood...." (9.20). In the end, all of the heavens and the earth are destroyed (Rev 21.1).

For Seneca and some other pagan Stoics, there is going to be a fiery conflagration in which the cosmos is temporarily destroyed, that is, recycled. Seneca describes this end time, "I am behold the rise and fall of future kingdoms, the downfall of great cities, and new invasions of the sea... know that nothing will abide where it is now placed, that time will lay all things low and take all things with it."[15] This includes "...places, countries, and the great parts of the universe. It will level whole mountains... it will drink up seas...."[16] There will be plagues, earthquakes and floods, which will kill all creatures. The fire will destroy all. The world will be blotted out in order to begin life anew. "... when it shall seem best to God to create the universe anew — we, too, amid the falling universe, shall be added as a tiny fraction to this mighty destruction and shall be changed again into our for-

---

[14]BJ VI.8.3, as quoted by S. Lachs, *A Rabbinic Commentary on the New Testament*, 419-421.

[15]Seneca, Moral Discourses, vol II, 95.

[16]Seneca, Moral Discourses, vol II, 95.

mer elements."[17] For many Stoics, the cycles of destruction and reconstruction are infinite in number.

---

[17]Seneca, Moral Discourses, vol II, 95,97.

Chapter 7

Arrest, Trial, and Crucifixion

Jesus says the owner, "will come and destroy the tenants and give the vineyard to others.
— Mark 12.9

My God, my God, why did you abandon me?
— Mark 15.34; The Scholars Bible

The death story of Jesus dramatizes the central message of the Gospel of Mark — Judaism is invalid and is to be replaced by Christianity. This theme is most clearly spelled out in the wicked tenant story of Mark 12 which we will now discuss before turning to the passion.

Tenant Story: Mark 12.1-12

Jesus relates that a man planted a vineyard, leased it to his tenants and moved away. When the harvest season arrived, the owner sent a slave to collect the owner's share of the produce, but the tenants beat the slave and kicked him out. The owner sent many others who were also beaten, ejected or killed. Finally, the owner sent his "beloved Son" whom the tenants killed, thinking that he had come for their inheritance. Jesus asks, what will the "owner of the vineyard do?" The owner, Jesus says, "will come and destroy the tenants and give the vineyard to others" (Mk 12.9). "They" realize the story was told "against them" (vs. 12) and want to arrest Jesus but are afraid of the crowd. ("They" apparently refers to the priests, scribes and elders at Mk 11.27.) The tenant story is loosely based on Isa 5.1-7, but Isaiah knows nothing of slaves or a son being murdered.

In Mark, the tenants are the Jewish people, those sent to collect the owner's share of the produce are the prophets of the *Jewish Scriptures*, and the son is Jesus. The meaning of the allegory is that the Jewish covenant is only temporary. It will be nullified by "the Jews" when they reject and kill the Son of God. They will then no longer be the people of God; the non-Jews will replace them and be given the vineyard, that is, the kingdom of God.

The tenant story is clearly a product of the early church.

The Passion: Mark 14.1-72

Most scholars concede that the accounts of the death story of Jesus in Matthew and Luke are dependent on Mark, but some argue that John's account of the passion is independent of Mark. Even an admirer of the fourth gospel like Raymond E. Brown writes, "It seems plausible to us that the *final writer* of Jn knew at least part of the Synoptic tradition, and, in particular, some written form of Mark."[1] Burton L. Mack in his influential *A Myth of Innocence*, argues that John's passion is dependent on Mark and is fiction.[2] Thus, we will rarely refer to John's late account of Jesus' passion.

In Bethany just outside of the holy city, at the home of Simon the leper, an unnamed woman anoints the head of Jesus, preparing him for his burial (Mk 14.3,8,32,33; Mt 26.12). In Luke the anointing occurs much earlier (Lk 7.36-50) and is not a funeral rite.

In the Synoptics the Pharisees play no role in the arrest, trial, and death of Jesus. John is in error when he depicts the Pharisees as playing a powerful role as there is no evidence that in 30 CE they had any such power. They are stand-ins for the Jewish rabbinical leaders of John's day (circa 100 CE).

---

[1]Brown, Raymond E. *New Testament Essays* (New York/ Ramsey: Paulist Press, 1965), 149.

[2]Mack, B., *Myth*, 225, fn 12.

The chief priests and scribes are looking for a way to arrest and kill Jesus (Mk 14.1). Judas goes to them and says that he wishes to betray Jesus; they are "greatly pleased, and promise to give him money" (Mk 14.10-11). Where did Judas and the priests meet? How did Judas know that these powerful priests needed help in arresting Jesus?[3]

Matthew begins the process of satanizing Judas by having him ask the priests for money, rather than the priests volunteering it as in Mark. In Matthew's gospel, Judas receives 30 pieces of silver. This is based on Zch 11.12-13, though Matthew wrongly attributes it to Jeremiah.[4]

Only in Matthew does Judas repent, return the money to the temple, and hang himself (Mt 27.1-10). This is derived from 2 Sam 12.23 and 17.23, where Ahithophel betrays David, and then hangs himself.[5] Acts contradicts Matthew by relating that Judas died when he fell and his body burst open (1.18) but oddly, in the Gospel of Luke, the supposed author of Acts is not aware of Judas' death by hanging, bursting, or any other method.

What reason is given for the betrayal of Jesus by Judas? In Mark none is given; in Matthew it is money. To Luke, it was not appropriate that the Son of God be betrayed for mere lucre, so Satan enters into Judas before the Last Supper (Lk 22.3) and during the Last Supper in John (Jn 13.26-27).

The Last Supper: Mk 14.17-25

In Judaism a festival is a time set aside to commemorate some historical event or religious concept. Passover celebrates the escape of the Hebrew people from Egyptian slavery under Moses' leadership. The four Gospels do not discuss the meaning of Passover or any other Jewish festival.

For John the Last Supper is characterized as a "supper," not a Passover meal (Jn 13.2,4). Jesus is executed the day *before* Passover in John and *on* the first day of the Passover in the Synoptics. John Chrysostom (fl 400 CE) was so anti-Jewish that

---

[3]Brown, Raymond E., *The Death of the Messiah*, 2 vols, 1994, New York: Doubleday, 1998, vol.1, 242.

[4]Crossan, John Dominic, *Who Killed Jesus?* (San Francisco: HarperSan-Francisco, 1995), 111.

[5]as quoted by Helms, R., *Gospel Fictions*, 116.

he thought the Jews postponed Passover for a day to allow them to kill Jesus!

In Mark, Jesus orders the disciples to prepare for the Passover meal. They do so on Thursday a little while before sunset (Mk 14.16), but Jesus would not have waited until it was this late, since in Jewish tradition, 15-30 days is recommended.[6]

Various kinds of food and drink are regarded as sacred and used in religious rituals. In the Jewish Scriptures, unleavened bread and wine are so used, but in Jewish tradition such rituals do not produce mystical effects. In some pagan magical papyri "the food is identified with the body and/or blood of a god with whom the magician is identified; thus the food becomes also the body and the blood of the magician; whoever eats it is united with him and filled with love for him."[7] Jesus, referring to the consumption of the bread and wine, says, "this is my body... this is my blood of the covenant..." (Mk 14. 22,24). Eating the blood of an animal is explicitly forbidden in the *Jewish Scriptures* and eating human blood and flesh, even symbolically, occurs nowhere in all of Jewish tradition.

The *Jewish Scriptures* are again handy for Mark as he creates the Jesus story. At the supper, Jesus says that his blood is poured out for many (Mk 14.14). "The righteous one, my servant, shall make many righteous, and he shall bear their iniquities... he bore the sin of many, and made intercession for the transgressors" (Isa 53.11-12), or vicarious atonement. Jesus removes the punishment for sin. This is not Jewish; in Judaism each person must atone for his or her own sins.

Jesus predicts that one of the twelve will betray him, the one who is dipping the bread into the bowl with him (Mk 14.20). The name of the betrayer is not given in Mark. Matthew identifies Judas, and adds that the Son of Man is fulfilling Scripture (Mt 26.24). It is, of course, unthinkable that the disciples do not condemn the one whom Jesus has just identified as the betrayer.

After the meal, Jesus and his disciples head for Gethsemane on the Mount of Olives (Mk 14.32) which is within sight of the temple in Jerusalem. On the way, Jesus miraculously predicts that his disciples will desert him, that Peter will deny him three

---

[6]Lachs, S., *Commentary*, 403-404.

[7]Smith, M., *Magician*, 122.

times before the cock crows twice, and that Jesus will meet them in Galilee (after his resurrection).

Mark again utilizes the *Jewish Scriptures*, in this case to prove that Jesus' disciples' desertion has been prophesied and is thus in accordance with the divine plan. Alluding to Zechariah Jesus says, "You will all become deserters; for it is written, 'I will strike the shepherd, and the sheep will be scattered'" (Mk 14.27; Mt 26.31; cf. Zch. 13.7).[8] Luke softens this harsh image of the disciples as faithless deserters, omitting the prophecy of their desertion (22.31).

In the garden, while the disciples sleep, Jesus experiences great mental agony although he assents to God's will, i.e., God's plan (Mk 14.34,36). L. Feder rightly points out that Hercules' most impressive trait "is his power to endure the burden of great toil and danger and agonizing personal sorrow"[9] and his gruesome death by fire.

The Arrest of Jesus: Mk 14.43-52

In the earliest gospel, Jesus and the twelve leave for the Mount of Olives after the Last Supper. At Gethsemane Judas pops up with the crowd coming to arrest Jesus even though Mark has not related that Judas had left the group. John knows this is a problem, and his Judas leaves during the supper at Jesus' command.

In Mark, the chief priest, scribes and elders *send* the crowd to arrest Jesus, but Luke has the aristocratic chief priests and elders personally appear to arrest Jesus! It is incredible that such powerful and aristocratic men would join the Temple police at night to make an arrest, and on Passover at that!

John's gospel fixes this. The dignitaries are not present. Rather, they have sent some officers to arrest Jesus. Yet, unbelievably, John has added a Roman captain with a cohort of 600 soldiers! This seems a bit much. At least the fourth gospel writer knew that only Roman authority could arrest a man for treason, that is, claiming to be a king.

---

[8]Helms, R., *Gospel Fictions*, 112.

[9]Feder, Lillian, *Apollo Handbook of Classical Literature*, 1964 (New York: Thomas Y. Crowell Company, 1970), 161.

Judas identifies Jesus with a kiss (cf. 2 Sam 20.9ff where Joab kisses Amasa just before killing him with a sword).

In Mark, a man near Jesus draws a sword and cuts off the ear of a slave of the high priest. Over time the gospel writers developed some of their fictional characters more fully. The name of the disciple (Simon Peter) and the name of the slave (Malchus) are finally revealed in John's gospel (18.10). Consider how much of Judas' story is lacking in the earliest account of Mark. He knows nothing about the 30 pieces of silver paid to Judas nor that he is a thief; he is not named at the Last Supper and Mark omits Judas' repentance and death. After the arrest of Jesus, Judas disappears.[10] In Matthew, Jesus says he could call on twelve legions of angels to protect himself if he desired (26.53); again demonstrating that Jesus is not accepting the divine plan against his will. He is fulfilling Scripture (Mk 14.49; Mt 26.56).

Mark says that at Jesus' arrest, "All of [the disciples] deserted him and fled," Mk 14.49-50 (cf. Isa 53.2,12), fulfilling Jesus' own prophecy.

Regarding the lack of historicity in the passion narratives, the reader should recall the number of miracles performed by Jesus. He miraculously predicts his arrest, the desertion of his disciples, Judas' betrayal, Peter's denial of Jesus, and his own trial, suffering, death, and resurrection. In addition, in John the arresting crowd miraculously falls to the ground. Also, the Johannine Jesus commands the authorities to let his disciples go, which fulfills Jesus' prophecy that he would not lose any of his disciples. (Presumably John means other than Judas!)

Did Judas Exist?

R.E. Brown in *The Death of the Messiah*, writes, "Judas is mentioned 22 times in the NT: Mark 3, Matt 5, Luke-Acts 6, John 8."[11] Judas is chosen as one of the twelve (Mk 3.19) and is not heard of again until 14.10-11 where he conspires to betray Jesus. He is not identified by name at the Last Supper in Mark.

The names, Judas, derives from the name of one of the twelve tribes of Israel, Judah, but R. Brown thinks the name is not

---

[10]Maccoby, H., *Myth*, 37.

[11]Brown, R., *Death*, vol 2, 1394.

suspect, though he grants that, *Judas* "is etymologically related to 'Jew'....."[12] (Greek *Judah*) and he concedes that Judas could be seen as the hostile "quintessential Jew," as Augustine does when he holds that Peter represents the church and Judas represents the Jews.[13]

W.B. Smith, G. Volkmar, and Hyam Maccoby, among others, have argued that Judas never existed. R. Brown[14] disputes this, but lists some of the arguments advanced for this thesis:

- the paucity of evidence in the *Christian Scriptures*;

- "John (the brother of James) is named more frequently than is Judas (30 times)... compared to 22" mentions of Judas;

- "the staged nature of the scenes" as at the Last Supper where each disciple asks if he is the one who will betray Jesus, Judas speaking last (Mt 26.21-25);

- Judas appears in a setting in which an earlier gospel does not have him, e.g., the anointing at Bethany (Jn 12.4-5);

- the conflicting accounts of Judas' death in Matthew and Acts.

R. Brown concedes that nearly all of the gospel evidence about Judas is unreliable, but wrongly insists on the historical existence of Judas.[15] We would add that Paul, writing before Mark, knows nothing of Judas.

We have to wait more than a hundred years after Mark's gospel (written about 70 CE or later) to find a mention of Judas outside the *Christian Scriptures*. Bishop Irenaeus of Lyons, writing about 180 CE, uses neither Matthew nor Acts in discussing Judas' fate, and the Bishop knows only that Judas was kicked out of office, not that he died.[16] It is only with Origen in the early third century that we find a writer who refers to Judas' death by hanging (Matthew), though he does not know of the alternative death by bursting (Acts). We do not find a reference to both of

---

[12]Ibid., vol 2, 1395.
[13]Ibid., vol 2, 1395.
[14]Ibid., vol 2, 1397.
[15]Ibid., vol 2, 1396-97.
[16]ANF, Irenaeus, *Against Heresies*, vol 1, 388.

the accounts of Judas' death in Matthew and Acts until the late fourth century CE.

Trial of Jesus by Jewish Authorities: Mk 14.53-65

Jesus is led to the (unnamed) high priest late on Thursday evening where "all the chief priests, the elders, and the scribes [are] assembled" (Mk 14.53-54). (The Sanhedrin never met at night; thus, Luke places the trial in the morning.)

In Mark, the "whole" Sanhedrin (all 71 members apparently) is "looking for testimony against Jesus to put him to death" (Mk 14.55). Matthew has the trial take place at the high priest's house, but the Sanhedrin was not convened there,[17] nor did the high priest preside over the Sanhedrin at this time.[18]

Against Luke and John, Mark and Matthew relate that some witnesses falsely charge that Jesus had said he would destroy the Temple, but their testimony is not in agreement and is dismissed (Mk 14.56-59; Mt 24.60-61). According to the Scriptures, at least two witnesses are required for a verdict in a criminal trial (Num 35.30; Dt 17.6, 19.15). Mark has no valid witnesses. Matthew adds the two witnesses.

The council finds no evidence against Jesus (Mk 14.55). Again, the *Jewish Scriptures* provide material for Mark's fictional portrait of Jesus, "the governors and satraps sought... to find... occasion against Daniel; but they found against him... no occasion" (cf. Dan 6.4 LXX).[19]

In Mark and Matthew at the end of the trial, Jesus is convicted of blasphemy, but claiming to be Messiah was not a crime. Could other charges have been leveled against Jesus? Some have suggested that Jesus' death could have been brought about because of his conflict with the Pharisees and scribes over ritual law, i.e., healing on the Sabbath, ritual washing of hands, etc. In Mark and Matthew, no such charges are raised, even though Jesus was tried in Jerusalem, the seat of what power the Pharisees had.

Also, criminal charges could have been brought by the Sanhedrin against Jesus since he attributed to himself divine char-

---

[17]Lachs, S., *Commentary*, 398.
[18]Lachs, S., *Commentary*, 419.
[19]Helms, R., *Gospel Fictions*, 118.

acteristics by allowing himself to be called *Lord* and claiming the authority to forgive sins and regulate the Sabbath, etc. If Jesus claimed to be the "only" Son of God in a literal, not metaphorical sense, this would be non-Jewish and perhaps a criminal offense.

At the trial, the high priest asks Jesus if he will defend himself, but he is "silent and [does] not answer," fulfilling Isa 53.7. The high priest asks, "Are you the Messiah, the Son of the Blessed One?" But how does the high priest know that any of the titles, *Messiah* (Christ), *Son of the Blessed, Son of Man, Son of God,* apply to Jesus? Jesus is called the "Son of God" by demons, but they are silenced at his command, and none of the people even suspect that these titles apply to him; at most, the people think Jesus is a prophet (Mk 8.28) or maybe one who cures illnesses or exorcises demons.

Asked if he is the Messiah, Jesus answers, "I am; and you will see the Son of Man seated at the right hand of Power, and coming with the clouds of heaven" (Mk 14.61-62), a union of Dan 7.13 and probably Ps 110.1.[20] Hearing Jesus' admission, the high priest tears his garments and judges that Jesus is guilty of blasphemy. The priest asks the Sanhedrin for its decision and "All of them [condemn] him as deserving death" (Mk 14.64). S. Lachs points out that the high priest "was not allowed to tear his clothes in mourning for the dead"[21] and probably he would not do so here either. He also points out that the rabbinic writers held that blasphemy could not be punished by a court, but only by God.[22] Some members of the Sanhedrin and some of the guards spit on Jesus and beat him (Mk 14.65), behavior hardly likely to occur during a meeting of this distinguished court.

The historical inconsistencies and implausibilities contained in the accounts of the arrest of Jesus and his trial before the council force us to agree with Burton L. Mack, John Dominic Crossan, and others that these events are fiction, a good deal of which has been constructed from passages in the *Jewish Scriptures.*

---

[20]Lachs, S., *Commentary*, 420.
[21]Ibid.
[22]Ibid.

Trial by Pilate: Mk 15.1-20

Mark relates that the whole council again meets, and then in broad daylight parades Jesus through the streets of Jerusalem bringing him to Pilate, the Roman prefect (Mk 15.2-20). It is still the Passover, a holy day on which work is forbidden. What happened to the idea of arresting Jesus secretly?

Mark does not tell us why Pilate is in Jerusalem. The elders, scribes and the whole council who brought Jesus to Pilate apparently stay, and yet Mark does not relate that anyone other than Pilate witnesses Jesus' trial (Mk 15.2-5). The prefect asks Jesus, "Are you the King of the Jews?" Jesus answers ambiguously, "You have said so." Mark says that the chief priests accuse Jesus of many things, but Jesus makes no response. Pilate is amazed at Jesus' silence, but he needn't have been astonished. Mark is again borrowing from the *Jewish Scriptures*. Isaiah 53.7 says, "He was oppressed, and he was afflicted, yet he did not open his mouth; like the lamb that is led to the slaughter...."

Suddenly a crowd pops up and asks Pilate to release a prisoner on the festival day as was his custom (Mk 15.8). (There was no such pagan or Jewish custom.) Pilate, based on Jesus' ambiguous answer and his silence, concludes that Jesus is innocent and offers to release Jesus, "the King of the Jews." But stirred up by the chief priests, the crowd demands that Barabbas, an insurrectionist and murderer, be freed instead and yells, "Crucify him!" Why is a murdering rebel freed? To keep the peace one assumes!

In Matthew, Mrs. Pilate needs even less evidence of Jesus' innocence than her husband. She has had a dream that Jesus is innocent, and sends word to her husband that he should have nothing to do with the death of this "innocent man" (Mt 27.19). Pilate washes his hands saying, "I am innocent of this man's blood..." (Mt 27.24). This is based on Deuteronomy 21.6-8, where the elders of the town wash their hands saying, "Our hands did not shed this blood." This practice is also found among the Greeks and Romans (cf. Virgil, *Aeneid* 2.719). The powerful prefect, Pilate, is portrayed as a strong and cruel official in the works of both Philo and Josephus. They know nothing of the weak and vacillating Pilate offered in the gospels of Mark, Matthew, and Luke.

In a passage that has caused much bloodshed, Matthew intensifies the guilt of all Jews throughout all time when he has the Jewish crowd cry out, "his blood be on us and on our children" (Mt 27.25). Compare this with Sam 1.16 where an Amalekite killed Saul at his own request and David says to the killer, "Your blood be on your head; for your own mouth has testified against you, saying 'I have killed the LORD's anointed [Messiah].'"

Did the Sanhedrin have the power to try Jesus for a capital offense? The first-century Jewish historian, Josephus (*Ant* 20.202-203), relates that a high priest convened the Sanhedrin and tried and executed some of his enemies. This was done between procurators. When the new one arrived in Jerusalem, the high priest was removed from office.

Luke and John know that the council could not try capital cases, which is why the third and fourth gospels omit the formal trial of Jesus by the Sanhedrin. In John, "the Jews" tell Pilate that Jesus is a criminal, and the prefect tells the chief priests to "judge him by your own law" (Jn 18.29-32). "The Jews said to him, 'It is not lawful for us to put any man to death'" (Jn 18.31). Did not the powerful Roman official know that under Roman law, only he could try and execute someone for a capital crime?

According to Mark after the murderer, Barabbas, is released, the Roman soldiers take Jesus away, mock and spit on him and strike him on the head (Mk 15.19,20; cf. Isa 50.6).[23] But a Roman governor would never have executed a man after publicly announcing his innocence. After the scourging by the Roman soldiers, Jesus is led away to be crucified, carrying his cross (Mk 15.20). In Mark, Matthew and Luke, a stranger, Simon of Cyrene, carries Jesus' cross part of the way to the place of execution.

It is unlikely that it was a Roman custom for the victim to carry his own cross. The condemned, especially one who had been flogged, would not have been physically able to carry a large and heavy cross, the vertical beam alone being about nine feet long. The upright beam of the cross was probably permanently embedded at the place of crucifixion, the cross beam being supplied at the time of execution.

---

[23]Helms, R., *Gospel Fictions*, 120, describes a similarity between Isaiah and the beating of Jesus before the Sanhedrin.

Why does John contradict the Synoptics by flatly saying that Jesus carries the cross by himself? Perhaps R. Helms is correct when he says that John may be attempting to counter the Gnostic claim that Jesus was not crucified, that instead Simon took his place on the cross.[24]

Mark uses *cross* in a metaphorical sense when he has Jesus say, "whoever wishes to follow me, let him deny himself, let him bear his cross and let him follow me" (Mk 8.34). Luke takes this saying of the early church too literally, and has Simon actually follow behind Jesus while carrying the cross (Lk 23.26).

To "bear your cross" is an ancient metaphor. The idea that a divinely inspired man or a demigod could be unjustly convicted and die on the cross was not alien to the Greco-Roman world. Martin Hengel in his book, *Crucifixion*, concedes that in Stoic thought "... an ethical and symbolic interpretation of the crucifixion was still possible." A staple of the ancient novel was the hero who barely escapes crucifixion.[25]   (For more on this see Chapter 9.)

The issue of who was present during the crucifixion again illustrates the confusion of the passion accounts in Mark and the other gospels. In addition to the centurion's presence at the crucifixion, Mark includes women, among whom Mark names Mary Magdalene, Mary the mother of James the younger and of Joses, and Salome (Mk 15.39-40). (Marks says these are the women who ministered to Jesus out of their own funds in Galilee, though up to 15.41 he has not mentioned any such women.) The disciples are not present.

Luke, against Mark and Matthew, says that the disciples did not desert Jesus at his arrest and claims that "all his acquaintances" are present at the cross (23.49). Luke is again rehabilitating the disciples. Only the late gospel of John relates that at the cross Jesus entrusts his mother to the care of the "disciple whom he loved" (Jn 19.26). But why is Jesus' mother not given into the care of her surviving sons?

---

[24]Wilde, Robert, *The Treatment of the Jews in the Greek Christian Writers of the First Three Centuries* (Washington, D.C.: The Catholic University of America Press, 1949), 153.

[25]Hengel, Martin, *Crucifixion* (Philadelphia: Fortress Press, SCM Press Ltd., London, 1977, Trans. from German ed. of 1976), 89.

Crucifixion: Mk 15.22-29

R. Helms' *Gospel Fictions* is helpful in examining Mark's use of the *Jewish Scriptures* in creating his fictional narrative.[26]

On the cross, Jesus is offered drink, "they gave him wine mixed with gall, but having tasted it he refused to drink" (Mk 15.23; Mt 27.34). Compare this with Psalms 69 (17), "they gave me also gall for my food, and made me drink vinegar..." (Ps 69 [70]:21). John fuses Ps 69 with Ps 51.7, and adds that Jesus is offered the wine on a branch of hyssop (Jn 19.21-30). John is heavily into the lamb of God imagery and hyssop was used for sprinkling the blood of the Passover lamb on the door posts of Jewish homes (Ex 12.21).[27]

Isaiah says that "... he was wounded for our transgressions, crushed for our iniquities; upon him was the punishment that made us whole..." (Isa 53.5; cf. Rom 4.25; 1 Cor 15.3). What Isaiah means by the "suffering servant" is the subject of much debate, but he certainly was not referring to Jesus or to a Jewish Messiah.

The soldiers cast lots to see who gets Jesus' clothing (Mk 15.24). "'they parted my garments... among themselves, and cast lots for my raiment' (Ps 21 [22]: 18 LXX)."[28] The seamless tunic in John (19.23) comes from Ex 28.32.[29] The gospels indicate Jesus' clothing is removed before the crucifixion (Mk 15.24). The Mishnah concludes that the inclusion of nudity in an execution would violate Jewish religious laws.[30] As Brown points out, nudity would cause conflict in the community which Rome was anxious to stabilize.[31]

According to Mark, a sign reading, "The King of the Jews," was affixed to the cross indicating the charge for which Jesus was executed (Mk 15.26; cf. Isa 53.12). R. Brown concedes that, "we have no evidence of the custom of affixing [a sign] to the cross."[32] And where is the sign located? Mark does not say; Matthew indicates that it is over Jesus' head; Luke has it over

[26]Helms, R., *Gospel Fictions*, 121.
[27]Ibid., 123.
[28]Ibid., 124.
[29]Ibid., 124-125.
[30]Brown, R., *John*, vol 2, 902.
[31]Brown, R., *John*, vol 2, 902.
[32]Ibid.

Jesus, and John, trying to smooth things out, says that the sign was "on the cross."

Those passing by the cross deride Jesus; they shake their heads and mock him, saying that he should save himself (Mk 15.29-30; cf. Ps 22.7). They say, "let us see whether Elijah will come to take him down" (Mk 15.36). Isaiah writes, "He was despised and rejected by others; a man of suffering..." (Isa 53.3; cf. Mk 9.12; 15.29-32).

Jesus is crucified along with two (unnamed) bandits, one on each side of him (Mk 15.27). The Psalmist writes, "For dogs are all around me; a company of evildoers encircles me" (Ps 22.16). Isaiah writes, "he poured out himself to death, and was numbered with the transgressors" (Isa 53.12; cf. Mk 15.27). Mark and Matthew describe those crucified with Jesus as *bandits*, a word which has strong political connotations. Luke, wishing to de-politicize Jesus' death, changes the word to *criminals* (Lk 23.32).

In Mark and Matthew, Jesus' despairing last words on the cross are, "My God, my God, why did you abandon me?" (Scholars Bible, Mk 15.34; cf. Mt 27.46; Ps 22.1). In Luke and John this is too much for their divine Messiah; they change the last words, removing Jesus' deficient faith. Luke's Jesus calmly commends his spirit to God (23.46). John's Jesus triumphantly proclaims, "It is finished" (19.30).

Epictetus wrote that since one's true ancestors are the gods, we should cheerfully be willing to die for God.[33] The pagan centurion at the foot of the cross after Jesus' death exclaims that Jesus was truly "God's Son" (Mk 15.41). Luke thinks it is too much that the pagan soldier would miraculously draw this conclusion and changes it to "Surely this man was innocent" (Lk 23.47).

The evangelists were children of their time. They believed, as did pagans, that miraculous events accompany the death of a great or divine man. Mark 15.33 records that the whole Earth was in darkness between noon and three on Friday afternoon. Some apologists say that this refers to an eclipse of the sun, but modern astronomy shows that no solar eclipse was visible from Judea at the time Jesus died in the early 30's CE. All of the Synoptics state that the curtain which closed off the inner

---

[33]Reale, G., 77.

Holy of Holies in the temple is torn in two. The divine presence has deserted the temple. The evangelists are supersessionalists. They claim that Christianity replaces Judaism.

Some conservative exegetes have tried to explain why Jews in the gospels are depicted as embracing the crucifixion, a Roman method of execution much hated in Jewish tradition. The apologists claim that Jews accepted crucifixion. But Paul Winter is surely correct when he says that we do not know of a "single instance [during the war, 66-70 CE] in which the Jewish guerrillas... resorted to the method of crucifixion in disposing of those who had fallen into their hands. Crucifixion was not a punitive measure used by Jews or adopted by Jewish judicial institutions at any time in history."[34] The Jews accept this cruel form of punishment because Mark wishes them to do so. He cannot make the representative of the pagans, Pilate, the murderer of Jesus.

Burial of Jesus: Mk 15.42-47

Mark relates that Joseph of Arimathea, a respected member of the council who was looking for the "Kingdom of God," "boldly" goes to Pilate and asks him for Jesus' body for burial (Mk 15.43). The problem is that Joseph, as a member of the Sanhedrin, must have voted to condemn Jesus, since Mark and Matthew relate that the vote of the council was unanimous. Luke can only weakly argue that Joseph had "not agreed to their plan and action" (Lk 23.51). As a known follower of Jesus, Joseph should have been arrested. Why wasn't he? And the disciples, too?

In Matthew, Jewish authorities request guards to watch over Jesus' tomb because Jesus said that he would be raised on the third day (Mt 27.64), but Jesus had predicted his resurrection only in private to his disciples. After Jesus is raised from the dead, the soldiers are bribed by the priests to say that Jesus' body was stolen while they slept. If Roman soldiers admitted they were asleep on duty, there would have been more crucifixions, and soon!

R. Helms correctly asserts that "... the [passion] accounts are... fiction, composed for theological purposes."[35]

---

[34]Winter, Paul, *On the Trial of Jesus*, Berlin: Walter de Gruyter and Son Co., 1961., 66.

[35]For more JS material in the passion see Helms, R., *Gospel Fictions*, 123ff.

Chapter 8

Resurrection

The women "fled the [empty] tomb...and they said nothing to anyone,
for they were afraid."
— Mark 16.8

The hero, thinking his wife is dead, comes to mourn, and finds the tomb
empty.
Ancient pagan novel.

The Empty Tomb: Mk 16.1-8

For the Greco-Romans, physical resurrection was seen as superstitious and repulsive. So, isn't Mark opposing pagan values when he states that Jesus is physically resurrected from the dead? Let us see.

According to Mark, after the Sabbath on Sunday morning Mary Magdalene and two other women travel to the tomb of Jesus in order to anoint his body with spices (Mk 16.1-2). They discover that the large stone that had blocked the entrance has been moved. They enter the tomb and are alarmed when they see an angel ("a young man") who informs them that the crucified Jesus of Nazareth has been raised. The angel orders them to tell Peter and the other disciples that Jesus will meet them in Galilee. Mark relates that the women fled the tomb in terror, "and... said nothing to anyone, for they were afraid" (Mk 16.8). It is widely accepted by scholars that the original version of Mark ends at 16.8 with the empty tomb, because Mk 16.9-20 appears only in very late manuscripts (fourth and fifth century). Thus, for Mark there is no physical resurrection. There are no appear-ances to anyone. Jesus' body has simply disappeared.

Nearly all serious scholars agree that the variant resurrection accounts of the gospels cannot be reconciled. A few examples of the inconsistencies involved will suffice to show why.

In Mark, Luke, and John, when the women (or a woman in John) arrive at the tomb, the stone has already been rolled away from the entrance. But in Matthew's account, when the women arrive, the stone is still in place and is rolled away by an angel of the Lord in their presence and that of the guards.

In Mark three women go to anoint Jesus' body, though earlier an unnamed woman has already anointed Jesus. In Mark and Matthew, Jesus appears first to Mary Magdalene and some other women. In Luke, Jesus appears only to men. In John, Mary Magdalene is alone when Jesus first appears to her. Matthew says that the women had come to "see" the sepulcher (Mt 28.1), and John gives no reason why Mary Magdalene comes to the tomb.

Ancient Greco-Roman Novels: Life after Death

The best place we know of to examine the basic issues concern-ing the historical Jesus is the scholarly *The Journal of Higher Criticism* edited by Robert M. Price. (See his website of the same name at www.atheistalliance.org/jhc/.) For the following, we have depended on Robert M. Price's book, *Deconstructing Jesus*.[1]

The plot line for certain ancient pagan novels, mostly of the Hellenistic period (ca 300-30 BCE), is primitive. In these novels, the wife or fiancé of the hero is in a coma and is prematurely buried. The hero, thinking she is dead, comes to mourn, and finds the tomb empty. He concludes that a god has taken his fiancé or wife to heaven because of her beauty.

In searching for her, the hero runs across a ruler who wants the heroine for himself and orders that the hero and those who stole the woman's corpse from the tomb be crucified. This being a romance novel, the hero survives. When the couple finally is reunited, they think at first that they are seeing ghosts.

---

[1]Price, Robert M, *Deconstructing Jesus* (Amherst, NY: Prometheus Books, 2000)., Ch 7, 213-221.

The similarities between Mark and, for example *Chaereas and Callirhoe*, are obvious:

- condemning the hero to be crucified;

- the entombment of the victim who is (apparently) dead;

- the removal of the stone;

- the empty tomb;

- the temporary inability of the lovers to recognize each other (in Mark, the women think that the angel is a ghost and in John, Mary Magdalene doesn't recognize Jesus at first).

There are parallels in other novels as well. Note that sometimes mistaken identity is involved, as in Achilles Tatius' *Leucippe and Clitophon*. This novel echoes the Gnostic accusation that Jesus did not die; another man takes his place on the cross. Also in this novel, a woman discovers on the third day that the tomb is empty. In the Latin novel, *The Golden Ass* by Apuleius (ca 123 C.E.), there are two scenes involving crucifixions, one of which involves the actual, if temporary, raising of a dead person.

In a fragment of Petronius's *Satyricon*, a woman decides to starve herself to death in her dead husband's tomb. Nearby, thieves are crucified. Guards are placed to keep other thieves from breaking into the tomb and removing the corpse. The woman is encouraged to eat proving that she is alive. Matthew, Luke and John provide witnesses to prove that Jesus has risen. In these pagan novels many people witness the empty tomb. As with Mark's gospel, these popular novels contain empty tombs, but this does not indicate physical resurrection.

Translation

In *The New Testament and Hellenistic Judaism*, an anthology edited by P. Borgen & S. Giversen, "Apotheosis and Resurrection," an article by Adela Yarbro Collins argues persuasively that the empty tomb in Mark "is shaped by Greek and Roman traditions of the translation and apotheosis of human beings."[2] Ac-

[2]Collins, A.Y., "Apotheosis and Resurrection," Borgen, Peder and Soren Giversen, Eds., *The New Testament and Hellenistic Judaism* (Peabody, MA: Hendrickson Publishers, Inc. 1995), 88-100.

cording to Ovid, Hercules' body was destroyed and he received a divine form, and Plutarch relates that Hercules' body disappeared. The *Jewish Scriptures* record that some people like Elijah, Enoch, Moses, and Melchizedek were translated, i.e., transformed after death not physically resurrected, and these Jewish figures are not depicted as becoming divine.[3]

Although Paul wrote in the 50's, only 10-20 years after the supposed death of Jesus (about 30 CE), his letters show no awareness of the empty tomb or anything else that would indicate a physical resurrection. Paul agrees with Mark – Jesus was not resurrected, but translated.

A.Y. Collins believes that the gospel of Mark ended at the death of Jesus on the cross;[4] there was no empty tomb and no resurrection of Jesus. Virtually all serious scholars think that the resurrection appearances included in Mk 16.9-20 were created from material extracted from the other gospels. For Mark, Jesus was transformed after death; he was translated, not resurrected. But what happened to his body? According to A. Y. Collins, when a person is translated, the body may remain behind or can disappear as in the case of Enoch, Elijah and Hercules.[5]

Mark, the earliest Gospel writer, indicates that Jesus is translated. Physical resurrection was developed by Matthew and Luke. Matthew indicates that Jesus was physically resurrected; the women take hold of Jesus' feet and worship him (Mt 28.9). Luke supplies more evidence of physical resurrection; Jesus shows the wounds on his hands and feet to the disciples, and points out that ghosts don't have flesh and bones. He then asks for food and eats a piece of fish (Lk 24.38-43). In John's gospel, Jesus eats food, appears in a closed room, and the doubting Thomas physically examines the wounds in Jesus' hands and side (Jn 20.26-27).

In the Roman world, it was required that witnesses testify to seeing the emperor's shade or soul ascending toward the heavens before the emperor could be deified. Not satisfied with witnesses to Jesus' resurrection, the author of Acts supplies wit-

---

[3]Maccoby, Hyam, *Paul and Hellenism* (Philadelphia: Trinity Press International, 1991. Vallentine, Mitchell & Co., Ltd., 1963.), 62.

[4]Collins, A.Y., 88.

[5]Ibid., 88.

nesses to Jesus' ascension, "When he [Jesus] had said this, as they were watching, he was lifted up, and a cloud took him out of their sight" (Acts 1.9; cf. Mk 16.19; Lk 24.50-53).

Lucian (120-185 CE) says that Hercules "was burned and deified on Mount Oetna: he threw off the mortal part of him that came from his mother and flew up to heaven, taking the pure and unpolluted divine part with him...."[6] (In Greco-Roman tradition the mother supplies the body; reason and virtue, etc., come from the father!)

Excursus: Zoroastrianism

Christian apologists, assuming that Christianity was a Jewish sect, suggest that we look to the *Jewish Scriptures* for the origin of the idea of resurrection. Yet the term resurrection appears rarely in the *Jewish Scriptures*. As the *Anchor Bible Dictionary* states, the term resurrection "...does not appear except in texts that are rare, obscure with regard to their precise meaning, and late."[7] Resurrection is not clearly mentioned until Daniel (ca 165 BCE). The usual biblical view is that the soul goes to Sheol after death.

Perhaps, then, we should look at the later Jewish writings of the Second Temple period (ca 200 BCE to ca 100 CE). The problem is that in Daniel and in pseudepigraphic literature such as 1 Enoch, Jubilees, 2 and 4 Maccabees, we find the concept of a *general* resurrection, not an *individual* resurrection, much less one where the Messiah is resurrected.

Eastern religions had for a long time influenced the Roman world. Zoroastrianism was widespread, especially in the eastern empire where Christianity originated. The idea of apocalyptism in Persian Zoroastrianism was taken over by ancient Judaism in the exilic period. By the sixth century BCE, Zoroastrianism had worked out its basic eschatology.

Some of the following items found in Zoroastrianism are also found in Christianity: the evil god, Angra Mainyu, or Ahriman (cf. Satan), rules a demonic world. Zoroaster teaches that after death the soul hovers around the body for three days before

---

[6]Boring, M., HCNT, 177, #242, Lucian in Hermotimos, or Concerning the Sects 7.

[7]Freedman, D., vol 5, 680.

going to its judgment. After the judgment, the soul goes to either heaven or hell, or an intermediate state, which we may call purgatory.

In Zoroastrianism, the cosmos lasts for twelve thousand years. There are three saviors who will follow Zoroaster, all born to virgins. Each savior's work lasts a thousand years, which reminds one of the thousand-year rule of Christ in *Revelation*. The third savior, Soshyant, overcomes evil and at the final judgment raises the dead (as Christ does in *Revelation*). Each individual is judged. The body and soul are purified and all (some in Christianity) are reunited with God. At this time the earth returns to its original perfection. Christianity is close to this latter idea in *Revelation* when, after people are judged, the cosmos is destroyed, a new heaven and a new earth are created, and the heavenly Jerusalem descends to the new earth.

We conclude that:

- The resurrection material in the gospels contains too many inconsistencies and contradictions to be harmonized.

- As time passed, the four gospels gradually eliminated the role of women as witnesses to the resurrection of Jesus.

- The idea of translation is more compatible with the pagan culture than with Jewish tradition. For Paul and Mark, Jesus is translated, but by the early second century CE, the idea of a physical or bodily resurrection became dogma.

- Physical resurrection was derived from Zoroastrianism.

Commentary on the Gospel of Mark: Conclusions

- Jesus is non-Jewish; he is grossly ignorant of Judaism and things Jewish..

- The Marcan Jesus is a radically anti-Jewish Christian; he is a supersessionalist, believing that Judaism is to be replaced by Christianity.

- Jesus' biography was created by the early church.

- His death story was written for theological reasons and is largely based on the *Jewish Scriptures*.

- Jesus fits better in a pagan, rather than a Jewish milieu. He is a pagan savior in Jewish dress. Mark's gospel is a fiction. It is a myth, and one that is not based on an historical figure.

That Jesus was non-Jewish needs to be emphasized. Virtually all modern scholars accept the gospels' portrayal of Jesus as a first-century CE Judean Jew. J.H. Charlesworth writes, "To me as a scholar *Jesus' Jewishness* seems redundant. Obviously Jesus was a Jew;..."[8] Cardinal Martini agrees, "In its origins Christianity is deeply rooted in Judaism... Jesus is fully Jewish, the apostles are Jewish, and one cannot doubt their attachment to the traditions of their forefathers."[9] All this is wrong. As we have shown, one *can* have serious doubts about Jesus' Jewishness, indeed about his very existence.

According to the Marcan Jesus, the Jews were the chosen people of God but they severed their covenant with God when they rejected and killed God's Son. Thus, non-Jews will replace them as the people of God. Christians have so interpreted the Gospels for nearly 2000 years and today conservative Christians, still faithful to the Gospels, preach this message of supersessionalism. Mark's gospel is, on a fundamental level, far too anti-Jewish to have been created in a Jewish milieu. Mark was created by the church, but who created the church? We will turn to this question in Chapter 10 of this book after exploring Paul's contribution to the creation of Christian orthodoxy. Chapter 10 will also deal with why Mark's Gospel contains both a low and a high Christology, that is, Jesus is depicted as both a fallible human failure and a divine-like being.

---

[8]Charlesworth, James H., *Jesus' Jewishness: Exploring the Place of Jesus within Early Judaism* (New York: Crossroad, 1991), 13.

[9]Martini, Cardinal Carlo Maria, "Christianity and Judaism: A Historical and Theological Overview," 19-34 in James H. Charlesworth, Ed., *Jews and Christians: Exploring the Past, Present, and Future* (New York: Crossroad Publishing Co. 1990), 19.

Part II

The Jesus and Paul Factions

Chapter 9

Paul, Jesus, and the Mysteries

Paul founded or joined a syncretistic mystery cult. He fused this cult with Gnosticism and stoic-cynicism, and added a Jewish veneer. Paul never knew the historical Jesus.
— Authors.

The Silence of Paul on the Historical Jesus

Traditional Christians hold that Paul's Christ is Mark's Jesus. In his letters, Paul appears to refer to the historical Jesus and his associates, Peter, James, etc. We will examine these supposed passages to see if he does, but first we will briefly consider the authenticity and integrity of Paul's letters as a whole.

Virtually all modern scholars believe that of the thirteen letters attributed to Paul, only seven are genuine: 1 Thessalonians, Galatians, Romans, 1 & 2 Corinthians, Philippians, and Philemon. Traditionally they are thought to have been written between 45 and 62 CE. These letters were edited, that is material was added to or subtracted from them as the needs of the church changed. In The Journal of Higher Criticism,[1] Hermann Detering briefly reviews some of the evidence offered by the Dutch school in the 19th-century as regard the integrity of the Pauline letters.

---

[1]Detering, Hermann, "The Dutch Radical Approach to the Pauline Epistles," *The Journal of Higher Criticism* 3 (Fall 1996),163-193.

There are a number of anachronisms in Paul's epistles. The highly-developed theology and international organization of the church which is apparent in Paul's letters assumes "*a longer period of incubation* and could not possibly have been arrived at within two decades" of Jesus' death[2] (Detering's ital.). Paul writes that he fought at Ephesus with wild animals (1 Cor 15.32),[3] but we have no evidence that Christians were fed to the lions until the letters of Ignatius of Antioch written about 117 CE, more than 50 years after Paul's death.

There are other problems with the Apostle's letters. Apologists argue that Paul wrote to individual churches, but 1 Corinthians is addressed to the church in Corinth at 1 Cor 1.2a, and to the churches "everywhere" at verse 2b. Also, scholars claim that Paul deals with specific problems of individual churches, but the subjects of his letters are universal in nature. The Apostle deals with faith versus works, morality, the theological meaning of Christ's crucifixion and resurrection; he writes of false apostles, false gospels and false "Christs," and of the end times, divorce, and ascetic practices, among other broad subjects. These topics are so general in scope, they could have been addressed to the church in general and at any time.[4]

Another problem with the historicity of Paul's correspondence is that the situation in which the letters were produced is confused. Often we do not know when or why Paul wrote a given letter, whether he is in prison or not, etc. Paul claims to be Jewish, but his letters "have in many places a completely non-Jewish character."[5] Van Manen argued that Paul was a "Gentile Christian."[6]

Nearly every subject that Paul writes about is treated in an ambiguous and often contradictory manner. For example, there have been two centuries of debate about who the opponents of Paul are in Galatians (54-55 CE). Some of the guesses are: 1) Jews, 2) Christians of Jewish background, 3) gentiles who observed the ritual laws of Judaism, 4) Gnostics of pagan back-

---

[2]Detering, H., JHC 3 (Fall 1996): 181.

[3]Detering, H., JHC 3 (Fall 1996): 190.

[4]Doughty, Darrell J., "Pauline Paradigms and Pauline Authenticity," *The Journal of Higher Criticism* 1 (Fall 1994): 112-113.

[5]Detering, H., JHC 3 (Fall 1996): 187, fn 66.

[6]Detering, H., JHC 3 (Fall 1996): 175.

ground, 5) Gnostics of Jewish background, 6) spirit-filled en-
thusiasts. Another problem with Galatians is that the accounts
of the Jerusalem meeting in Galatians 2 and Acts 15 have long
been seen as inconsistent and even as fiction.

1 Corinthians (ca 56-57 CE) is believed by some scholars to
be a composite document that has been interpolated.[7] (Most
think that this is true of 2 Corinthians as well.)

Jesus

Now let us see what, if anything, Paul knows about the historical Jesus or his disciples or family. We will focus primarily on
Galatians and 1 Corinthians, as these two letters contain virtually all of Paul's supposed references to the historical Jesus, his
brother, and his disciples.

Paul says that Jesus was "born of a woman, born under the
law" (Gal 4.4), but the Apostle supplies no historical detail. Paul
knows of no birthplace and Jesus could have been born a hundred years before Paul. In his single reference to Jesus' ancestry, Paul says that Jesus "was descended from David according
to the flesh," i.e., was of Jewish royal descent [Rom 1.3-4). We
agree with Earl Doherty, (The Jesus Puzzle) that Paul does not
know that Christ is a descendant of David. We think the entire
passage (1.1-7) is an interpolation, since Paul nowhere else gives
any historical data as to the ancestry of Jesus; and Rom 1.1-4
contains much detail unknown to Paul and Mark, the earliest
Christian writing. Many scholars have questioned the integrity
of these two passages from Galatians and Romans.

Paul describes the "Lord's Supper" at 1 Cor 11.23-29, but
the integrity of this passage has been much questioned. Jesus'
words, "this is my body and blood... Do this in remembrance of
me,..." are closest to Luke's account, but Paul died about 64 CE,
25 years before Luke wrote his gospel (ca 85 CE).

Paul's most detailed depiction of the human nature of Jesus
occurs at Phil 2.6-11. This pre-Pauline hymn says that Jesus
Christ "was in the form of God,... that he emptied himself, taking the form of a slave, being born in human likeness... he hum-
bled himself, and became obedient to the point of death — even

---

[7]Brown, Raymond E., An Introduction to the New Testament (New York: Doubleday & Company, Inc., 1997), 512.

death on a cross." Finally, the hymn adds that after Jesus' death, God "exalted him" above all others. There is nothing else in the "genuine" letters of Paul about a divine figure descending from heaven and becoming human. The hymn was inserted by later editor.

Again, Paul refers to Jesus' crucifixion but gives no historical detail. At I Thess 2.14-15 Paul says that "the Jews" killed "the Lord Jesus." R. Brown lists some arguments that scholars have given against the Pauline authorship of this passage which Brown, nevertheless, accepts as genuine:[8]

1. The letter gives a second thanksgiving, indicating that the letter is a composite.

2. The passage says that Jews are "enemies of the human race," a common pagan slander.

3. The letter states that divine wrath has overcome the Jews, a reference to the first war with Rome (66-70 CE) which occurred after Paul's death about 64 CD..

Against Brown, most modern scholars have concluded that 1 Thess 2.14-15 was inserted by the early church. Earl Doherty in *The Jesus Puzzle*, lists some of the scholars who have found this to be so:[9]

- Burton Mack, *Who Wrote the New Testament?* p 113;

- Wayne Meeks, *The First Urban Christians*, p 9, n 117;

- Helmut Koester, *Introduction to the New Testament*, vol. 2, p 113;

- Pheme Perkins, *Harper's Bible Commentary*, p 1230,1231-2;

- S.G.F. Brandon, *The Fall of Jerusalem and the Christian Church*, p 92-93;

- Paula Fredericksen, *From Jesus to Christ*, p 122.

---

[8]Brown, R., *Introduction*, 463.

[9]Doherty, Earl, *The Jesus Puzzle* (Ottawa, Canada: Canadian Humanist Publications, 1999), 299.

- We would add J.D. Crossan who, in *Who Killed Jesus?*, asserts that the whole account of the Jewish trial is fiction.

Paul knows that Christ was "resurrected," but he does not know where or when. In 1 Corinthians, Paul preaches that, "Jesus died, was buried, and raised on the third day according to the scriptures" (15.3-4), a passage which many scholars think is a creedal formula added by a later editor. Following this is Paul's list of resurrection appearances: Jesus first appeared to Cephas and the twelve (1 Cor 15.5); then to the 500 disciples (vs. 6); then to James and all the apostles (vs. 7); and finally Jesus appeared to Paul himself (vs. 8). Scholars have found many problems with this passage, one of which is that it is inconsistent with the other passages dealing with Jesus' resurrection appearances as described in the four Gospels and in Acts of the Apostles.

As we saw in Chapter 8, Mark does not assert that Jesus physically arose from the dead, but was translated or transformed after death. This is also true of Paul elsewhere in his letters.

Paul's Savior is not Mark's historical Jesus, but the Christ, a triumphant and divine figure of glory from the mythic past.

Peter

There is evidence in Paul's letters of general conflict within the early church. Paul warns his flock to watch out for those who would cause dissensions and offenses contrary to what they have learned (Rom 16.17). He says there are false apostles who preach a perverted gospel and "another Jesus" (2 Cor 11.4-8,13-14,22-33; Gal 1.6-9); he warns that they "will pay the penalty" (Gal 5.10,12).

Paul did not know Peter. His references to Peter, John and James were added by an editor in an attempt to prove that the Apostle knew these associates of Jesus, thus establishing a link between Paul's Christ and the historical Jesus.

Paul says that his gospel "is not of human origin; for I did not receive it from a human source, nor was I taught it, but I received it through a revelation of Jesus Christ" (Gal 1.11-12). He says, God "set me apart before I was born" and revealed "his Son to me, so that I might proclaim him among the Gentiles" (Gal

1.15-16; 1 Cor 1.1; 2 Cor 1.1, Phil 1.1, Rom 1.1). Paul writes that after his conversion, he "did not confer with any human being, nor did [he] go up to Jerusalem to those who were already apostles before [him], but... went away at once into Arabia...." (Gal 1.16-17). In about 40 CE, three years after his conversion, Paul says he visited Cephas for fifteen days in Jerusalem and also saw James, the Lord's brother (Gal 1.19), but Paul insists that he did not receive any part of his gospel from Peter, Cephas, James, or any other human being.

Fourteen years after his first visit to Jerusalem, Paul writes that he received a revelation from God and returned to Jerusalem, this time with Barnabas and Titus (Gal 2.1-2). Paul meets privately in Jerusalem with the supposed "acknowledged leaders" (James, Cephas and John) but he again flatly asserts that they "contributed nothing to me," (Gal 2.2,6). In other words, Paul insists that his gospel did not come from Jesus of Nazareth through his disciples or his brother. Even if Peter is Cephas, Paul does not indicate that he received truth from him. Also, it would be anachronistic for Paul to refer to Peter as Cephas, since Peter was not called by this name until John 1.42, written decades later (ca 100 CE) after Paul's death about 64 CE.

An editor of Galatians attempted to convince his readers that Paul knew Peter by having Paul explicitly say that Peter's gospel, as well as his own, came from God (Gal 2.7-8). We do not find any reference to this passage in Christian writings until Irenaeus about 180 CE. Tertullian, writing about 207 CE, knows about the Jerusalem leaders shaking hands with Paul, i.e., approving of his mission to the non-Jews, but he knows nothing of the statement that Peter's gospel came from God.[10]

Paul says he met with James, whom he describes as the brother of Jesus, but only once, at Gal 1.19; a passage which many scholars are wary of. After all, we last saw James in Mark's gospel, where he is depicted as an unbeliever who thinks that Jesus is crazy and maybe even possessed by Satan, and yet at the meeting in Jerusalem we find James is apparently the head of the church of Jerusalem!

Paul knows nothing about the disciples as depicted in Mark and the other gospels. Paul never even hints that Peter, James

---

[10]Ibid., 296-297.

(excluding the brother passage), John, or anyone else ever met Jesus, much less that they were his disciples.

Finally, how can it be argued that Paul knew of the historical Jesus when he is wholly ignorant of the Marcan traditions about Jesus? Here are some items found in Mark's gospel but omitted in the Apostle's letters. Paul knows nothing of Bethlehem, Capernaum, Galilee, Nazareth, or Judea. Paul does not know of Judas, John the Baptist, Herod Antipas, the high priest, or Pontius Pilate. He doesn't mention the Sadducees, the Sanhedrin (which supposedly tried Jesus), the scribes, or even that Jesus had disciples. He uses the word Pharisee only once (referring to himself at Phil 3.5). The apostle refers to Cilicia but fails to mention the city of Tarsus, though Acts says that he was born there. He mentions the Twelve one time at 1 Cor 15.5, but does not associate the twelve with the apostles. A major element of Judaism which he ignores is the temple in Jerusalem, having only a single reference to it at 1 Cor 9.13.

Also, Paul does not know of Jesus' special teachings, his cures, exorcisms, or other miracles. Paul knows only of Jesus' ahistorical death. He does not know of an historical man who lived and died in Palestine about 30 CE. Paul's Christ was crucified in the mythic past and returned to life as a god, a spiritual Christ. His Christ is in the tradition of pagan gods like Osiris, Dionysius, Mithras, and Hercules, all of whom suffered and died, were transformed after death, becoming divine. For additional analysis of the silence of Paul about Jesus, see Earl Doherty *The Jesus Puzzle*.

Paul and Pagan Syncretism

If Paul was unaware of the existence of Jesus, and thus was not a Christian, what was his religion? To answer this, one must fully appreciate the powerful and pervasive syncretism of the ancient Roman world that produced him.

Merriam-Webster's Collegiate Dictionary defines the verb *syncretize* as an "...attempt to unite and harmonize especially without critical examination or logical unity."[11] The word has been applied to both religion and philosophy.

---

[11] *Merriam-Websters Collegiate Dictionary*, Merriam-Webster, Inc., 1998, 1873.

Religious syncretism is ancient, existing long before Paul. In Herodotus' *History of the Persian Wars*, (5th cent. BCE), we find Greeks identifying the Egyptian Osiris with the Greek god Dionysus.[12] When Rome conquered Greece, the chief god, Zeus, was identified with the chief Roman god, Jupiter. In the syncretistic world of the first century CE we should not be surprised to find that Paul's religion was a mix of many elements. We shall examine that religion, but first a note on Paul's Jewishness.

Paul Was Not a Jew

Paul claims to be Jewish but 90 percent of the evidence of his Jewishness is contained in Acts of the Apostles, a late fantasy that we need not consider here. Paul does not know Hebrew. He writes in common Greek (Koine), and quotes the Greek translation of the *Jewish Scriptures* (the Seventy), and when it differs from the Hebrew, he always prefers the Greek. Paul was neither a rabbi nor a Pharisee nor a Jew. (See H. Maccoby's books *The MythMaker* and *Paul and Hellenism*.)

Today Greco-Romans are described as anti-Jewish and Paul is said to love Jews. But as we shall see, pagan opinions of Jews and those of Paul are virtually identical.

Both Paul and paganism wrongly claimed that Jews hated non-Jews. At 1 Thess 2.15-16, Paul claims that "the Jews" are against humanity, and have attempted to prevent him from saving non-Jews. Posidonius (fl 2nd and 1st cent. BCE) says that pagan writers believed that Jews disliked non-Jews. He says that Jews would neither eat with "gentiles" nor "...show any good will towards them."[13] Diodorus says that the Syrian king should "wipe out the Jews completely" on the ground that they look upon all non-Jews as their enemies. He says Moses "ordained their misanthropic ways."[14] Apollonius Molon (fl 1st cent. BCE) reproaches the Jews for hatred of non-Jews, intolerance, super-

---

[12]Griffiths, J. Gwyn, "Hellenistic Religions," 237-258 in *Religions of Antiquity*, Ed. Robert M. Seltzer, 250.

[13]Wilde, R., 45.

[14]Feldman, Louis H, *Jew & Gentile in the Ancient World*, (Princeton, NJ: Princeton University Press, 1993), 10.141 Diodorus, Historical Library 34.1.1-4.

stition, and the immorality of the law.[15] Tacitus claimed that Jews held as sacred all things which were impure to the (non-Jewish) Romans.[16] According to Josephus, Apion insisted that by law Jews kidnapped a non-Jew each year and sacrificed and ate him and swore an oath of hostility to the Greeks.[17] Later Christians adopted this slanderous myth and believed it to be true until the 19th century CE!

Paul was pro non-Jews. He writes that Israel has been blinded until the fullness of the gentiles is come in (Rom 11.19,21). Jews are the enemies of God in order to save non-Jews (Rom 11.28-30). "I am an apostle to the gentiles in order to make my fellow Jews jealous and thus save some of them" (Rom 11.1-14); but only some. Loyalty to the ethnic or religious traditions of one's ancestors was greatly valued by the Romans, so here and elsewhere Paul claims that he has strong feelings for his "kinsmen," and indeed he does love "some" of the Jews — if they become non-Jews, i.e., Paulinists.

Some pagans wrote that Jews were atheists because they rejected the pagan gods. Some charged Jews with worshiping idols; Plutarch implies that Jews worship a donkey[18] and Tacitus explicitly says so.[19] Some scholars say Paul argues that Jews were idolatrous (see Gal 4.9) and accuses Jews of unbelief in that they reject the "true" God and his son, Jesus.

Feldman writes, "Circumcision was regarded by the Greeks and Romans as a physical deformity and hence, like others who had various deformities, circumcised men were not permitted to participate in the Olympian Games."[20] Paul warns the Philippians to "Beware of the dogs, beware of the evil workers, beware of those who mutilate the flesh!" (circumcise, Phil 3.2).

Seneca, Tacitus and Suetonius all ridiculed the observance of the Jewish Sabbath, as did Horace, Ovid, the satirist Persius,

---

[15]Wilde, R., 46-47.

[16]Feldman, Louis H., and Meyer Reinhold, Eds., *Jewish Life and Thought Among Greeks and Romans* (Minneapolis: Fortress Press, 1996), 385, 10.144, Histories 5.4.1.

[17]Feldman, L., *Jewish Life*, 386, 10.148 Apion *History of Egypt* cited by Josephus, *Against Apion* 2.91-6.

[18]Feldman, L., *Jewish Life*, 363, 10.81 Plutarch, *On Isis and Osiris* 31.

[19]Feldman, L., *Jewish Life*, 363, 10.82 Tacitus *Histories* 5.4.2.

[20]Feldman, L., *Jewish Life*, 377.

Plutarch, etc.[21] So does Paul. He rejects Jewish dietary law, which was viewed derisively by Greco-Roman writers. Plutarch writes about the Jews "honoring the pig."[22] Juvenal says that Jews feel "merciful" toward pigs.[23] Paul asserts that observing ritual law contributes nothing to salvation.

The Apostle to the "gentiles" insists that the law causes sin. He says the law was given to Jews because they were morally degenerate.[24] No Jewish thinker would condemn the ritual or ethical law by characterizing it as non-efficacious, as Paul does.[25]

A number of texts in which "the Jews" are spiritually blinded appear in Paul's letters, and Acts. often they depend on Isa 6.9-10:

The Lord orders the prophet Isaiah to tell

> "this people: 'Keep listening, but do not comprehend; keep looking, but do not understand.' Make the mind of this people dull, and stop their ears, and shut their eyes, so that they may not look with their eyes, and listen with their ears, and comprehend with their minds, and turn and be healed [saved]."

The authors of the *Christian Scriptures* tear this passage from its historical context. Isaiah is labeling the inhabitants of the Northern Kingdom of Israel as faithless. He is not rejecting all Jews for all time.

In the *Jewish Scriptures*, God at times spiritually blinds people in order to accomplish his purposes. In Exodus, for example, God hardens the Pharaoh's heart or that of the Egyptians. Sometimes the king himself is hardened (Ex 8.32; Ex 4.21, 10.20). God's purpose is accomplished, e.g., the King's army pursues the Israelites into the Red Sea and drowns (Ex 14.17), thus freeing the Jews from slavery.

The following passages illustrate how the early church explained why Jews rejected Jesus and the Kingdom of God, i.e., the church:

---

[21]Feldman, L., *Jewish Life*, 366.

[22]Feldman, L., *Jewish Life*, 374, 10.109 Plutarch *Festal Questions* 4.4-5.3.

[23]Feldman, L., *Jewish Life*, 377, 10.114 Juvenal *Satires* 6.160.

[24]Downing, F. Gerald, *Cynics, Paul and the Pauline Churches: Cynics and Christian Origins II* (New York: Routledge, 1998), 69.

[25]Downing, F., 62.

- In Rom 11.25, Paul states that part of Israel has been hardened "until the full number of the Gentiles has come in." The agent seems to be God (cf. 2 Cor 3.14; Heb 3.7-8, 4.7; and Mk 7.6-7).

- Paul argues that the gospel is "veiled to those who are perishing" (2 Cor 4.3). Unbelievers have been blinded "by the god of this world [Satan]... to keep them from seeing the light of the Gospel" (2 Cor 4.4)

- At Acts 28.25-28, Paul describes the Jewish heart as having grown dull; their ears do not hear, eyes do not see, etc. Jews have blinded themselves.

- At Rom 9.16, 18-20, Paul asserts that whether one is saved or not depends on the mercy of God. He writes that it is God who "hardens the heart of whomever he chooses" (vs. 18). Paul discounts human will or exertion. He writes that people say that if God blinds people, why does Paul find fault with unbelievers? Paul answers that human beings are not to argue with God. God has made us the way we are and we have no right to complain; that is like the pot criticizing the potter.

- At Rom 11.7-8, Paul argues that the elect have received salvation. The Apostle then paraphrases Isa 6.9-10, "God gave them a sluggish spirit, eyes that would not see and ears that would not hear, down to this very day."

Why does the early church depict Jesus as teaching that Jews are spiritually blinded by God? Paul in Acts spells it out, "Let it be known to you then that this salvation of God has been sent to the Gentiles; they will listen" (Acts 28.28). The mission to the Jews, if there ever was one, had failed. The church needed to explain why few Jews converted to Christianity. Note that no mission to Jews is related in Paul's letters, but only in the late fantasy, Acts, where the mission to "the Jews" fails.

From the preceding, one can see that Paul shares anti-Jewish views very similar to many pagan writers. Paul is hardly pro-Jewish or anti-pagan. R. Ruether writes, "For Paul, there is, and has always been, only one true covenant of salvation." And this covenant was "given *apart from the Law*, to Abraham and now [is] manifest in those who believe in Abraham's spiritual son, Christ. The people of the Mosaic covenant do not now and never have had any way of salvation through the Torah itself."[26] Jews can only be saved by becoming non-Jews, a view with which many pagan writers would agree.

While Greco-Romans like Tacitus were quite anti-Semitic, Paul is even more so. Why is this? Paul must make sure that Greco-Romans do not mistakenly believe that he is accepting Judaism as the true religion. Many pagans were certainly critical of Judaism, but Paul invalidates it, replacing it with Paulinism, that is, proto-Christianity.

Stoic-Cynicism

If Paul was a pagan, why did he embrace a belief in only one true is God? Many ancient Greeks and Romans rejected polytheism, including Plato and Aristotle, the Stoic-Cynic philosophers, and others.

Diogenes the Cynic "...expressed contempt for the Eleusinian mysteries... his teacher Antisthenes, who attacked all religious conventions including the belief in a multitude of gods, maintained that there existed one God beyond all visible phenomena."[27] The Sophist and atheist, Protagoras, said, "I am unable to know whether [the gods] exist or do not exist, nor what they are like in form; for the factors obstructing knowledge are many: the obscurity of the subject and the shortness of human life."[28]

For Epictetus, the Cynic is a mediator between god and humanity (cf. 2 Cor 2.17 to 3.9).[29] The Cynic is a representative of god who has been sent by Zeus to humans to teach them how to live (cf. Gal 1.1).[30]

Chrysippus, head of the Stoic school in 232 BCE, used allegory or symbolism in an attempt to prove that Homer and Hes-

---

[26]Ruether, Rosemary Radford, *Faith and Fratricide: The Theological Roots of Anti-Semitism* (1974). (New York: The Seabury Press, 1979), 106.

[27]Griffiths, J., 253.

[28]Griffiths, J., 252-253.

[29]Boring, M., HCNT, 446, #721, Epictetus, *Discourses* 3.24.64-65.

[30]Boring, M., HCNT, 459, #753, Epictetus, *Discourses* 3.22.23.

iod were actually Stoics.[31] The Stoics rearrange "the letters in the name of the goddess Hera (ERA) [giving] the word for air (AER)."[32] Similarly, Paul (and Jesus) rejects the literary meaning of the *Jewish Scriptures*. Interpreting them symbolically enabled Paul to "prove" that the *Jewish Scriptures* predicted long ago that Jesus Christ would be crucified, etc.

Seneca says, "What is my object in making a friend? To have someone to be able to die for, someone I may follow into exile...."[33] Some parallels from Paul are: Gal 5.14 says love your neighbor; Rom 12.14, bless those who persecute you. Note, however, that Paul is not as universal as some think, "Do not be unequally yoked together with unbelievers" (2 Cor 6.14-17).

Seneca says that the slave "has the same good sky above him, breathes as you do, lives as you do, dies as you do...."[34] He also says, "treat your inferiors in the way in which you would like to be treated by your own superiors."[35] Plutarch (45-125 CE) says we should give good for evil.[36] Paul says to "overcome evil with good" (Rom 12.17,19-21).

Epictetus says we are "all children of god, and that god is the father of gods and men...."[37] Paul teaches that God is our father (cf. Rom 1.7; Rom 8.15-17; 1 Cor 8.6; Gal 4.6; Mk 11.25).

Seneca writes that one should love one's country, father, and wife.[38] He writes that the wise man "remains self-content even when he marries, even when he brings up his children."[39] He would rather not live at all than to give up human companionship. Of Musonius Rufus (30-101 CE) it was said, "...he is the clearest of any ancient writer on the equality of man and woman (Frgs. Nos 3 and 4); he believed marriage to be a complete partnership" with sex being confined to marriage for the purpose of

---

[31]Ferguson, Everett. *Backgrounds of Early Christianity*, 1987 (Grand Rapids: W. B. Eerdmans Publishing Co, 2nd Edition 1993), 334.

[32]Ferguson, E., *Backgrounds*, 336.

[33]Seneca, *Letters*, Letter 9, 50.

[34]Seneca, *Letters*, Letter 47, 93.

[35]Ibid.

[36]Boring, M., HCNT, 384, #609, *Moralia*, "Common Quote on Compliancy" 13.

[37]Epictetus, *Discourses* 1.3.1; 11.

[38]Seneca, *Letters*, Letter 88, 153.

[39]Seneca, *Letters*, Letter 9, 52.

procreation.[40]

Epictetus states that men get married and beget children because they wish to be happy.[41] Family feeling is good and natural.[42] He also says that the man who commits adultery destroys friendly feeling toward his neighbor, destroys friendship, and the country[43] (cf. 1 Cor 6.9-12, adulterers will not inherit the kingdom). Seneca writes that many things encumber us in our pursuit of wisdom, the "body, property, brother, friend, child, and slave...."[44] The fundamental purpose of philosophy is to learn how to live.[45]

Judaism celebrates life. Stoic-Cynics varied as to the value they put on marriage but most accepted it if it was not perceived as an obstacle to the pursuit of wisdom.

Paul's view on marriage is similar to Stoic-Cynics in that he does not explicitly forbid it, yet like some Stoics, he writes that people should be celibate as he is (cf. 1 Cor 7.7-8), that a man should not touch a woman (1 Cor 7.1). He also says that women should be silent in church and subordinate to the husband, a view that most Greco-Romans would find acceptable.

Stoicism and Paul share the same terminology, "Spirit, conscience, *Logos*, virtue, self-sufficiency, freedom of speech, reasonable service, etc."[46] Also, both believe in the human tendency toward evil (stronger in Paul), the need for self-examination, human kinship with the divine, denial of the world's values, and emphasis on inner freedom from external circumstances.[47]

Other parallels between Paul and the Stoic-Cynics are:[48]

- Both the Stoic-Cynics and Paul believed in proselytizing, and posited founders whose teachings were passed down.

- Both saw externals as neutral or indifferent, playing no role in salvation. Examples of externals would be marriage,

---

[40]Ferguson, E., *Backgrounds*, 344.

[41]Epictetus, *Discourses* 1.11.3; 28.

[42]Epictetus, *Discourses* 1.11.17; 30.

[43]Epictetus, *Discourses* 2.4.1-3; 82.

[44]Epictetus, *Discourses* 1.1.14; 6.

[45]Seneca, *Letters*, Letter 55, 107.

[46]Ferguson, E., *Backgrounds*, 346.

[47]Ibid., 346.

[48]Ibid., 346.

wealth, politics, as well as whether one was a Greek or barbarian, slave or free, male or female.

- Both argued that one must not fear death or suffering in the pursuit of truth.

- Both thought of conscience as the source of ethical truth.

In general, Paul was heavily influenced by the ideals of the pagan ethicists, "especially by the Cynic-Stoic synthesis of popular philosophy" (cf. Gal 5.19-23).[49] "Seneca's sentiments have more nearly approximated Christian teaching than those of any other classical philosopher. Tertullian described him as 'always our Seneca' (*On the Soul* 20),"[50] though, of course, the letters supposedly written by Paul and Seneca to each other are bogus.

The fundamental difference between Paul and the Stoic-Cynics is that the latter sought virtue in this world, while Paul sought salvation in the next world. For Paul, life begins after death.

So Paul's ethics were a syncretistic mix of Stoicism and Cynicism, but what of his views on salvation? Were they, in fact, Jewish or Christian?

Gnosticism

To Paul's syncretistic soup, we must add a large measure of Gnosticism. Gnosticism existed in the Roman Empire by the first century CE.[51] J. M. Robinson dates it to this century or earlier.[52] A number of scholars concede that incipient Gnosticism coexisted with Christianity's beginnings.

In Gnosticism, souls (sparks) have been expelled from heaven (the *pleroma*) and are trapped in the flesh,[53] i.e., bodies.[54] The gnostic savior, a spiritual being, descends from the heavenly hierarchy and imparts *gnosis* (mystical knowledge) to the elect

---

[49]Boring, M., HCNT, 474, #782.

[50]Ferguson, E., *Backgrounds*, 343.

[51]Cohn-Sherbok, D., 56. In the description of Gnosticism that follows, we have relied on this book.

[52]*Interpreters Dictionary of the Bible, The: An Illustrated Encyclopedia* (Nashville: Abingdon Press, 1962) Supplemental Volume, 364.

[53]Maccoby, H., *Paul*, 188.

[54]Maccoby, H., *Paul*, 187.

(*pneumatics*) which enables them to be reunited with God. Some souls can be saved by the elect; others are doomed. When enough sparks have returned to God, the material cosmos will collapse back into chaos.

Hyam Maccoby in *Paul and Hellenism*[55] identifies some elements common to Paulinism and Gnosticism. The rulers of the cosmos are evil spiritual entities (*archons*) and the purpose of the Savior's mission is to break the power of these evil forces which are led by the demiurge (Satan), and save the elect. Both Gnostics and Paulinists believed that humans fell from grace, from innocence to irredeemable sin; they are cut off from the true God and can only be rescued by a divine redeemer.

In ancient Judaism there was no such radical alienation from God. The sin of Adam and Eve simply explains why God's children do not live in Paradise, why men must labor to make a living, and women must give birth in pain. After Genesis, the *Jewish Scriptures* rarely refer to the Eden story. Judaism does not require a divine redeemer.

Additionally, both Paulinism and Gnosticism admired figures in the Jewish Bible who are non-Jewish, for example, Abraham, Seth, Enoch, and Melchizedek. According to Paul, all of the Jewish prophets thought that Judaism was only temporarily valid.[56] Against Exodus, Paul asserts that the law was given to Moses not by God, but by angels who also authored it.[57] (The Greek word *diatageis* in Galatians 3.19 means ordained not transmitted.[58]) Similarly, for the Gnostics the law was composed and delivered by the evil demiurge, not by God.

Paul obliterates the literal text of the Jewish Bible by allegorizing it, turning the Bible into a Paulinist anti-Jewish book.[59] Similarly, Gnostics turned "bad guys" into the good Gnostics, e.g., the snake in Eden is the cosmic savior. Plato (428-349 BCE) pointed out that pagans allegorized their sacred myths and writings. Plato's Socrates says, "these fine poems are not human...," "the poets are merely the interpreters of the gods,..."[60] The edi-

---

[55]Maccoby, H., *Paul*, 186.
[56]Maccoby, H., *Paul*, 188.
[57]Maccoby, H., *Paul*, 41.
[58]Ibid.
[59]Maccoby, H., *Paul*, 51.
[60]Boring, M., HCNT, 460, #754, Ion 534 E.

tors of HCNT assert that Paul "totally agrees" with the pagan idea of inspiration (cf. Gal 1.1).[61] H. Maccoby concludes that Paul is "close to the Gnostics in his view of God, Satan and Torah."[62]

As regard anti-Jewishness, the Gnostics on the whole did not view the Jews as evil incarnate but as simply spiritually ignorant.[63] However, they opened the doors for diabolization of the Jews by Christians, e.g., Jews are the people of the devil (cf. Jn 8.44).[64]

The Mysteries

Another major influence on Paul were the mysteries, or savior religions.

In the mystery cults, a savior god or one close to him or her dies and is brought back to life. Members of the cult undergo sacred secret rites, e.g., baptism and sacred meals. Through these rites they receive benefits such as health, protection from drowning at sea, or bliss after death and some argue that they achieve immortality. Momigliano writes that the "Imperial cult and [the mysteries] are, in fact, two of the most important features of Roman religion in the imperial period."[65]

From the 6th century BCE in the Greek world there were local mystery cults that, like the Christians, included women, foreigners, and slaves, and which, as E. Ferguson grants, may have involved the concept of an afterlife.[66] The mysteries "became truly universal after the conquests of Alexander, being expressly made available to citizens of the Roman Republic and then the empire."[67]

Orpheus

The mysteries each had their associated myths. Orpheus was initiated into the Samothracian Mysteries and descended into

---

[61] Ibid.

[62] Maccoby, H., *Paul*, 52-53.

[63] Maccoby, H., *Paul*, 37.

[64] Ibid.

[65] Momigliano, Arnaldo, "Roman Religion of the Imperial Period," in *Religions of Antiquity*, Robert M. Seltzer, Ed., 222.

[66] Ferguson, E., *Backgrounds*, 236-237.

[67] Ferguson, E., *Backgrounds*, 238.

the land of the dead, attempting to rescue his wife Eurydice. He was killed by the women of Thrace.[68] Some said that he instituted the mysteries; in one tradition, the soul of Orpheus was taken to the Elysian Fields (heaven) and brought out the secrets of how to reach the land of the blessed.[69]

Eleusinian Mysteries

In the myth of the Eleusinian mystery, Kore, the daughter of the grain goddess Demeter, is kidnapped by Hades and taken to the underworld, the land of the dead. After Demeter negotiates with Zeus, Kore is allowed to spend part of the year on earth with her mother, thus benefiting humanity by preserving the agricultural seasons. Demeter assures her initiates of happiness after death. This mystery cult predates Jesus and Christianity by about 600 years.

Dionysius

The cult of Dionysius was widespread during the Roman imperial period. In its myth Zeus inadvertently kills his human consort, Semele, with a lightning bolt which makes their unborn son, Dionysus, immortal. Dionysius engages in missionary activity from Greece to India preaching that he is an Olympian god. He and his followers are persecuted. Like Osiris he is hacked to pieces but is brought back to life by Zeus. Later the son travels to the underworld, bringing his human mother's shade back from Hades[70] (cf. Jesus' trip after his death to preach to the spirits in prison 1 Pet 3.19-20). Dionysius then ascends to Mount Olympus to take his place among the immortals.

Isis

By 38 CE the cult of the Egyptian goddess, Isis, had spread throughout the empire. (The following information on Isis is from E. Ferguson.)[71] She describes her powers in an inscrip-

---

[68]Grimal, Pierre, *The Penguin Dictionary of Classical Mythology* (London: Penguin Books, 1991), 315-316.

[69]Ibid., 316.

[70]Ferguson, E., *Backgrounds*, 238-241, 243.

[71]Ferguson, E., *Backgrounds*, 253, 255, 297-300.

tion (1st cent. BCE to 1st cent. CE). In part Isis says that she is the oldest daughter of Cronus, and the wife and sister of Osiris who was dismembered by their brother, Set, who scatters his body throughout Egypt. Isis brings Osiris back to life. She is called God by women. She divided earth from heaven, created the courses of the stars and the sun and moon, made justice strong, coupled woman and man, set the pregnancy of women at nine months, ordered that children will love their parents and that humans will love truth. She punishes those who act unjustly. Lucius in *The Golden Ass* says that Isis ruled the world, and was the savior of the human race. Devotees of Isis repented of their sins. Meals were commonly associated with mysteries, and in the cult of Isis, the elect are "saved," i.e., given immortality or bliss after death.

Adonis and Attis

E. Ferguson tells us that the Phoenician deity, Adonis, is killed by a wild boar and brought back from the dead. In the late second century BCE, the cult of the Phrygian gods, Cybele and Attis, was received in Rome by the Senate. Attis dies a violent death.[72] R. Price writes of an "... effigy of ashes crucified to a pine trunk. On the third day he would be proclaimed gloriously risen from the dead..."[73]

Mithras

According to Ferguson, Plutarch says that, as a mystery, the Persian cult of Mithras existed by 67 BCE. A shrine to Mithras was built into Hadrian's wall (d 135 CE) in what is now England. Like Jesus in the birth stories of Matthew and Luke, Mithras was not a product of sexual union. He slays the sacred bull from whose blood all life arises and is associated with the sun god, Sol, with whom he shares a sacred meal. As with the deified Roman emperors, Mithras ascends to heaven. E. Ferguson concedes that the Persian god offered a form of salvation to his adherents. An inscription in Rome says, "You saved us by shedding the eter-

---

[72]Ferguson, *Backgrounds*, 260, 264.
[73]Price, *Deconstructing Jesus*, 87.

nal blood."[74] Many scholars assert that Mithrans believed that baptism of blood made them immortal. This cult like that of Isis had "a supernaturally sanctioned ethic" comparable to Christianity.[75]

Hercules

Hercules was one of the most universally worshiped gods in the Greco-Roman world and was said to have been initiated into the Mysteries of Eleusis. He was punished by Zeus for freeing Prometheus, who had saved humans by providing them with fire. Hercules, after much physical and psychological suffering, climbed onto his burning funeral pyre on Mount Oetna, and was raised to the heavens on a cloud, becoming one of the immortals.

Asclepius

Asclepius, the god of healing, raised so many people from the dead that Zeus killed him, after which he was divinized.[76]

Price writes that, "the Greco-Roman world was up to its hips in mystery gods."[77] We would add that it was also up to its hips in other gods who were associated with violent death and helping humankind.

* * *

Like most pagan saviors, Paul's Christ is an ahistorical being. The apostle gives no date or place for Jesus' birth, crucifixion, or death. His Christ is crucified and translated in the mythic and vague past where, according to Greco-Roman tradition, Hercules, Asclepius, Kore, Dionysus, Osiris, Mithras, and many other demigods and gods died violent deaths.

The savior gods were associated with the translation of a person after his or her death. H. Maccoby writes,[78] "Dionysius... is brought to life again by Rhea. Adonis... is raised on the third day. Baal... comes back to life. Attis, after dying of his wounds,

---

[74]Ferguson, *Backgrounds*, 271, 274, 275.

[75]Ferguson, *Backgrounds*, 281.

[76]Ferguson, *Backgrounds*, 281.

[77]Price, *Deconstructing Jesus*, 88.

[78]Maccoby, H. *Paul*, 71.

comes back to life and dances. Osiris... is put together again and revived, after which he becomes a god. In Mithraism, the bull killed by Mithras was not itself resurrected, but it provided life, through its body and blood, for the whole created universe." Paul makes many references to the raising up of Jesus. But as Maccoby points out, there is no reference to a dying Messiah in Judaism until the Talmud of the fifth century [b. Sukkah 52a]. "[W]e find the antecedents of the death of Christ,..."[79] in the mystery religions.

Most scholars vigorously deny that Paul was a member of a mystery, arguing that the myth of dying and rising gods did not predate Paul. But R. Price asserts that perhaps the strongest argument "that the resurrection of the Mystery Religion saviors preceded Christianity is the fact that ancient Christian apologists did not deny it! Only so would they have reached into left field for the desperate argument that Satan *foreknew* the resurrection of Jesus and counterfeited it *in advance*, so as to prejudice pagans against Christianity as a mere imitative also-ran, which is just what they thought of it"[80] (Price's italics). That is, Satan supplied myths of the dying and rising gods so that pagans could later claim that Christians copied the Mithran and other pagan savior cults!

H. Maccoby concludes that, "In general, we must conclude that there is good evidence that the concept of salvific revival or resurrection of a violently-dying god existed in the mystery cults by the time of Paul."[81]

Mysticism

The mysteries associated death and mysticism. Paul alludes more than 150 times to a mystical union of himself (or other believers) and Christ or the Holy Spirit. "I have been crucified with Christ" (Gal 2.20). Many have put on Christ and been baptized in him (Gal 3.27). At the Lord's Supper, many participate in the body and blood of Christ (1 Cor 10.16). Paul says that believers will unite with Jesus Christ in the resurrection (Rom

---

[79]Maccoby, H. *Paul*, 63, 65.
[80]Price, R., *DJ*, 91.
[81]Maccoby, H., *Paul* 73.

6.5).[82]

Paul believes that God caused Jesus' death, "as a sacrifice of atonement by [Jesus'] blood" (Rom 3.24-25). In the religions of Cybele and Mithras, atonement was through the blood of sacrificed animals.[83] The Mithran initiate is reborn for eternity (cf. Rom 6.1-10).[84] According to Apuleius (ca 125 CE), a mystical union with the deity occurs during a religious meal (cf. Mk 14.22-25).[85] He also says the cult of Isis involved an ecstatic state on the part of the initiate, visions of hell and heaven, and contact with the realm of the dead. Lucius says that he was "given new life [immortality]" by Isis (cf. Rom 5.1-11).[86]

Organization

Lastly, we must note the similarity of the organization of Paul's churches with that of the voluntary associations common in the Greco-Roman world. Under Augustus, many private groups met under the auspices of a god; these voluntary associations (funeral societies, the mysteries, etc.) were regulated by the Roman senate.[87] Note the organizational features held in common by the mysteries and the early Pauline churches.

Compare the inscription from Philadelphia in Asia Minor (Lydia, late 2nd cent. or early 1st cent. BCE) with Gal 3.28; 5.13 to 6.10.[88] Here are some of the traits shared by voluntary associations and the Paulinists:

1. the "equality of women and men, slaves and free is emphasized";

2. hospitality and belonging to a community;

3. the group is morally elite, superior to the culture at large;

---

[82]Boring, M., HCNT, 361-362, #570.

[83]Boring, M., HCNT, 353, #558.

[84]Boring, M., HCNT, 364, #572.

[85]Boring, M., HCNT, 149, #194, Apuleius, *The Golden Ass*, 11.

[86]Boring, M., HCNT, 361-362, #570, Apuleius' *Metamorphose* (*Golden Ass*),11.6,21-25.

[87]Beard, Mary, John North and Simon Price, Eds., *Religions of Rome Volume 2: A Sourcebook* (Cambridge: Cambridge University Press, 1998), 292-294, 12.2.

[88]Boring, M., HCNT, 416-418, #670.

4. anti-magic, as in Acts Ch 8, also see 13.8-12, 19.18-19, Rev 9.21;

5. lists of activities that are considered immoral;

6. a strict code of sexual ethics;

7. an oath at time of initiation;

8. the presence of the god in the cult (cf. Mt 18.20).

The Statutes of the Associates of the Worshipers of Diana and Antinous (2nd cent. CE)[89] are important for understanding the Christian Eucharist texts:

1. the common meal is religious;

2. the organization revolves around the meal;

3. there was conflict involved during the celebration of the meal;

4. the meal is institutionalized as in 1 Cor 11. In paganism, "The festive meals serve as memorials to important events in the lives of honored figures in the life and history of the group."[90]

Conclusions: Chapter 9

R. Price is correct in pointing out that it is difficult for Christian apologists "to see extensive and basic similarities between [the mysteries] and the Christian religion. But somehow Christian scholars have managed not to see it, and this, one must suspect, for dogmatic reasons. Those without such a Maginot Line mentality have less trouble."[91]

Many Christian writers refuse to equate Paul's religion with the mysteries and Gnosticism. R. Price rightly asks, "how close does a parallel have to be to count as a parallel? Does the divine mother have to be named Mary? Does the divine child have to be

---

[89]Boring, M., HCNT, 468-469, #771.
[90]Boring, M., HCNT, 427, #687.
[91]Price, R., DJ, 88.

named Jesus?"[92] Does the dying and rising god have to mirror Christ in every respect? Must members of every mystery cult believe that she or he will be physically resurrected in a manner identical to that of the early Christian church? We need not assert that Paulinism was a mirror image of a pagan mystery, as did F. Cumont, Richard Reitzenstein, and R. Bultmann in the early 20th century. Paul's religion was a kaleidoscope, reflecting many syncretistic elements of the Greco-Roman world; it was not an identical copy of any particular pagan religious phenomenon. The Pauline church played a creative role in the development of its own myth.

R. Price asks whether when members of the mystery cults were mystically united with the god, was "it possible for them to participate in the god's death and resurrection in some way and so gain an immortality like his? Sure it was. And the Mystery Religions were born."[93] And so was Paulinism.

Paul was a pagan. He was not a Jew and he was not a Christian in that he did not know of, or follow, the Marcan Jesus. His cult was not based on the life and teachings of an "historical" Jesus. In the next chapter we will see who created Jesus and why and who equated him with Paul's ahistorical Christ, thus creating orthodox Christianity.

---

[92]Price, R., *DJ*, 89.
[93]Price, R., *DJ*, 87.

Chapter 10

Who Created Jesus?

Pilate asked [Jesus], "What is truth?"
— John 19.38

Paul's "belief that he received the myth from the heavenly Jesus himself has obscured his own role in creating it."
— Hyam Maccoby, Paul and Hellenism.

In Part I of this book we showed that Mark's Jesus was a literary fiction and in Chapter 9 we demonstrated that Paul, supposedly the earliest literary witness to Jesus, was not aware of the existence of Mark's historical Jesus. If Jesus was an imaginary figure, who invented him? The Paulinists, the followers of Paul, created Jesus. We will now turn to how and why they did so.

As we saw in Part I, Mark's Gospel was layered. The first layer, proto-Mark, was followed by a second layer, Mark 2. Together these layers make up the earliest gospel, that of Mark. In proto-Mark, Jesus is not divine, but merely a man, one who wrongly believes that he is the Messiah King. This Jesus feels pity, anger, compassion, and other human emotions as we can see in what follows.

- Before Jesus receives the Spirit at his baptism by John, one assumes that he had only ordinary human abilities, as is shown by the fact that he performs no miracles until after his baptism (Mk 1.9-10).

- In the story about Jesus' true family, he disowns his mother, brothers and sisters (Mk 3.20 1, 31, 35).

151

- Jesus is fatigued as he is found sleeping during the storm he is about to still (Mk 4.38).

- He does not have infinite power at his disposal as the power flows out of Jesus in the story of the woman with the hemorrhage. Also he is not omniscient; he has to ask who touched his robe (Mk 5.30-34).

- The lack of faith among the people in Jesus' hometown (which amazes him), makes him unable to do any wonders other than cure a few sick people (Mk 6.5-6).

- Jesus expresses disappointment when the Pharisees ask for a sign (Mk 8.11-12).

- He is indignant when the disciples do not want him bothered by parents seeking a blessing for their children (Mk 10.13-14).

- In Jerusalem, he expresses great anger at those carrying out the normal business of the temple (Mk 11.15-16).

As to whether Jesus and his disciples believe that he is a royal Messiah, consider the following passages in proto-Mark:

- Peter and the other disciples believe that Jesus is "the Messiah" – a king (Mk 8.27-33) who will usher in the reign of God.

- At Mk 10.35-41, James and John, the sons of Zebedee, ask that they be given the highest positions in Jesus' kingdom when he comes to "his glory." The other ten disciples are angry for they, too, expect that Jesus will be the head of an earthly kingdom.

- As Jesus exits Jericho, a blind beggar addresses him as "Son of David," one of the signs Christians believed identified the Messiah, although Jews held no such belief by 70 CE (Mk 10.48).

- Upon entering Jerusalem (Mk 11.8-11), Jesus is greeted as a king.

- Later, in the garden before his arrest, Jesus, realizing he is not going to become a king, is distressed, agitated and sorrowful and asks God to "remove this cup from me" (Mk 14.33-34).

- At his trial before the Jewish Council, Jesus acknowledges that he is the Messiah (Mk 14.61).

- Before Pilate, Jesus does not deny that he is King of the Jews (Mk 15.2ff). Later in Mark, the inscription on the cross charges that Jesus claimed to be "King of the Jews" (Mk 15.26).

In Mark, Jesus is depicted as a faceless and failed Messiah. He is not a triumphant instrument of God who consciously ushers in the divine rule, but a failed messianic claimant who thought that God would make him king of Israel. He dies of a cross in despair, crying out "My God, my God why did you abandon me?" (Scholars Bible Mk 15.34).

Nor is Jesus alone in his faithlessness. Proto-Mark depicts Jesus' disciples, his mother, brothers, and sisters as faithless. His family thinks he is crazy or perhaps possessed by Satan (Mk 3.21, 31-32). Judas betrays Jesus. Peter and the other ten disciples all desert him when he is arrested. During Jesus' trial before the Jewish Council, Peter denies three times that he knew Jesus. Unlike the later Gospel of Luke, none of the disciples are at the cross when Jesus is crucified. The disciples are shown as faithful after Jesus' resurrection but, as we explained in Chapter 8, Mark originally had no resurrection scenes.

This earliest layer of the Gospel, proto-Mark, was not threatening to the Paulinists who created it. For them, Paul, not the faithless Peter, remained "the Apostle." Truth came from Paul's mystical union with Christ, not from the earthly Jesus through Peter. The faithless relatives and disciples of Jesus did not threaten the apostle's leadership. Paul's divine and triumphant Christ is not threatened since he is not identified with proto-Mark's Jesus, a messianic failure.

Why did the Paulinists create a failed Messiah? Paul asserts that God has a covenant with Jews and He does not break His promises. But, non-Jews cannot be saved until God's covenant with the Jews is broken. When God presents to them a royal claimant, a messianic king, the Jewish leaders reject him, engineering his death – the Jewish covenant with God is broken. As Matthew spells out in the "Great Commission" Jesus tells the disciples to teach all nations – non-Jews. Thus, Paul and the Jesus of proto-Mark are quite compatible.

But, when Mark 2 was added to proto-Mark producing the current Gospel, this Gospel threatened many in Paul's Church. The Jesus of Mark is now divine. Like God, he forgives sins, regulates the Sabbath, walks on water, and calms the sea. He raises the dead. He three times predicts in detail his own death. Jesus is aware of God's plan and consciously and deliberately executes it. Mark 2 (the current Mark), as most scholars agree, adds that Jesus predicts his own suffering and death. After Peter angrily reprimands Jesus for predicting that the Messiah-King will suffer and be killed, Jesus calls Peter "Satan," and strongly condemns him for his unbelief. In short, in the first layer of Mark, Jesus is not conscious that part of his mission is to go to Jerusalem and die.

In Mark, Jesus no longer merely predicts that the mysterious *Son of Man* will come in the future, nor that he himself will become this figure after his death. Now, during his lifetime, Jesus is the *Son of Man*, the *Son of God. Messiah* is now interchangeable with these divine terms. The title *Christ* becomes his last name. In Mark 13, Jesus tells the disciples to teach all nations, thus threatening Paul, the apostle of the Gentiles.

Matthew and Luke continued to rehabilitate Jesus and Peter. In the birth scene in Matthew, Jesus' mother, Mary, goes from thinking he is crazy (Mark) to a pious figure, a proto-Christian. In Matthew and Luke, Jesus is divine from birth and in John's Gospel, he is divine before the cosmos was created (through him); "... the Word was with God, and the Word was God." (Jn 1.1, 3). Peter replaces Paul as the founder of the Church. Matthew's Jesus says he will build his church upon this rock, that is Peter's faith. Jesus replaces the heavenly Christ of Paul. In the resurrection appearances in Matthew, Paul's leadership is challenged when such glory is given to the chief disciple of Jesus, Peter.

By the end of the first century CE, the church was polarized. There were now two groups, the Jesus and Pauline wings, each defending its own faith and founder. Those that stayed with Paul's ahistorical and spiritual Christ made up the Paulinist wing. The supporters of the historical Jesus made up the Jesus wing.

What is the evidence that the church was polarized into these two wings? When we look at the church writings that appeared between Paul (d. ca 64 CE) and Justin (fl ca 150 CE), we find they reflect two traditions:

1. the Pauline tradition as seen in Paul's letters, the pseudo-Pauline letters, and the writings of Ignatius – which do not focus on the historical Jesus;

2. the Jesus tradition as reflected in the Gospels and in the writings of Justin Martyr who is unaware of Paul, Ignatius and other writers in the Pauline tradition.

In reviewing the Paulinist literary tradition, we find that Paul's letters, aside from the interpolations that we discussed in Chapter 9, know nothing of an historical Jesus who died on a cross in Jerusalem. Paul knows only of a demigod who was crucified in the mythic past and transformed after death into a spiritual Christ. In this mythic past, many pagan gods had lived, died and come back to life. The pseudo-Pauline letters, too, (Ephesians, Colossians, 2 Thessalonians, 1 and 2 Timothy, and Titus) are unaware of the historical Jesus except for a bare reference to Pontius Pilate in the late and fraudulent 1 Timothy (6.13) which was probably written about 150 CE.

1 Clement (ca 95 CE) briefly refers to Peter and Paul as "illustrious apostles," indicating that the Jesus and Pauline traditions were united, i.e., that Paul's Christ is Mark's historical Jesus. This letter is unsigned and the earliest manuscript is late 4th century CE.

Bishop Ignatius (d ca 117 CE) mentions Peter and Paul only once as apostles in his letter to the Romans at 4.3. No other early Orthodox Christian author knows of a church tradition uniting both Peter and Paul until the end of the second century (Irenaeus and Tertullian).

Bishop Ignatius appears to know the Jesus tradition when he mentions Jesus' virginal conception, his crucifixion under Pontius Pilate and his resurrection but, according to many critical scholars, these historical references are part of a creedal formula added to Ignatius's writings at a later date. He has no knowledge of the birth stories of Jesus contained in the Gospels of Matthew and Luke. Indeed, Ignatius shows no awareness of the existence of any written gospel.

We will now deal with the Pauline letters and Acts of the Apostles that depict both Peter and Paul as operating in a united church, allegedly in the first century CE.

As to the Council meeting in Acts 15.6-29, surely Robert M. Price is correct when he asserts that this meeting is an insertion that attempts to prove Peter and Paul were harmonious fellow apostles.[1] The passage was added to attempt to prove that the Marcan historical Jesus, represented here by Peter, and the Pauline ahistorical Christ are the same personage. Acts of the Apostles, as John Knox demonstrated in *Marcion and the New Testament*, reached its final form by the second half of the second century CE. One can reject this late date for Acts, but how then could one explain why no one refers to this fantasy before Irenaeus (ca 180 CE), 95 years after its alleged composition by Luke in about 85 CE?

The second tradition, championed by the Jesus wing, is anchored in the four Gospels, supposedly written by about 100 CE. The writings used by the apologists to show that the apostolic writers of the second century embraced the gospel tradition are those of Justin Martyr (fl ca 150 CE). Justin quotes a variant form of Matthew's birth narrative but he uses Isaiah 7.14, not the birth stories in Matthew or Luke, to prove that Jesus was conceived by a virgin. Although Justin quotes Jesus (or "the Lord") and he knows of Pilate, the crucifixion, etc., Justin's knowledge of Jesus' life is sketchy. In any case, he certainly ignores Paul and his letters. He does not refer to the pseudo-Pauline letters, or the letters of Ignatius, i.e., the Pauline literary tradition, though he was writing nearly 100 years after the last letters of Paul were written in the early 60s CE.

In summary, by the end of the first century CE the church was divided into the Pauline ahistorical wing and the gospel or historical Jesus wing. Ignatius knew only the Pauline wing, and Justin knew only the Jesus wing (variant Matthew). In short,

---

[1]Price, Robert M., "Apocryphal Apparitions: 1 Corinthians 15:3-11 as a Post-Pauline Interpolation", at *The Journal of Higher Criticism* 2, Fall 1995, 95.

there is no definitive evidence before Marcion (ca 145 CE) that any Christian writer embraced both the Pauline and Jesus traditions. There may have been a movement which attempted to unify the Jesus and Paul traditions, but the evidence is thin. If the apostolic fathers knew of a dual tradition, they did not choose to reflect that knowledge in their writings. Tertullian says in *Against Marcion* that there was a Canon uniting the Gospels and Paul before Marcion. There is very little evidence to support the existence of a united church before Irenaeus (ca 180 CE).

But what united the Jesus and Pauline wings, producing a single canon and a single, unified church? Probably the answer lies in the work of the wealthy Gnostic Marcion (ca 144 CE).

Marcion traveled from Pontus (in modern Turkey) to Rome, joined the church there and was kicked out about 144 CE as a heretic. He founded many Marcionite churches across the Roman Empire. Marcionism threatened to split the church. Marcion denied both the Jewishness and humanity of Jesus. He severed any connection between Christianity and Judaism. The canon that Marcion created rejected the *Jewish Scriptures*, and omitted any mention of things Jewish in his version of Luke, the ten Pauline letters which he accepted as valid, and in his own writings. He asserted that the "cruel" God of the *Jewish Scriptures* and the "loving" God of his *Christian Scriptures* were not the same God. Marcion's ahistorical and bodiless savior was compatible with Paul's ahistorical, spiritual Christ, but nevertheless, Marcionism threatened to sever the Jesus wing from the polarized church. Thus, Marcion stimulated the formation of a united church which identified the historical Jesus with Paul's ahistorical, divine Christ, and formed a Canon – Paul's letters, the Gospels, etc., in the process.

Who reconciled the two wings? The centrists, or moderates, did so. By 180 CE, Bishop Irenaeus knows of the spiritual Christ of Paul and the historical Jesus of the Gospels; for him they are one and the same. Irenaeus copiously quotes the *Jewish Scriptures*, the Pauline corpus, the pseudo-Pauline letters, the gospels, and Acts (mostly the first half). He struggles mightily to pull the Pauline and Jesus wings together, forcefully insisting that the church had never been divided, that it came unified from God. He asserts that the canon had from the beginning contained only four gospels since there are only four principal winds, four faces of the cherubim, etc.[2] He writes that, "the very ancient, and universally known church (was) founded and organized at Rome by the two most glorious apostles, Peter and Paul."[3] But no writings reflect any such tradition before him, other than the interpolated letter, 1 Clement, the letters of Ignatius, and Acts of the Apostles, which we have discussed above. One truth, united from the beginning.

Christianity began with Paulinism. Its apostle was Paul who supposedly experienced a mystical union with a spiritual Christ who died in the mythic past and was then glorified. Mark took the Pauline Christ and historicized him, the centrists produced a unified orthodoxy. The divinized human Jesus of Mark caught on, leaving the Gnostics far behind. A god-man who recently lived on earth differentiated Christianity from all other mystery religions and from Gnosticism.

The polarized wings of the church had struggled with Gnosticism, the popular Mysteries, Jews, Stoic-Cynics, and "heretics." In the end, Irenaeus and the other centrists triumphed, but only at a great cost, namely the sacrifice of the original religion, Paulinism. The founder, Paul, was reduced to a mere apostle, one who was soon to be eclipsed by Peter. The centrists accepted Mark's historicization of Paul's mythic Christ and the religion became "orthodox" Christianity.

Jesus Christ was declared God at the Council of Nicaea in 325 CE.

---

[2]Irenaeus, *Adv. Haer.* Bk. 3, Ch 11 in ANF vol 1, 428.

[3]Irenaeus, *Adv. Haer.* Bk. 3, Ch 3 in ANF vol 1, 415.

Appendix A

Early Jewish and pagan references to Christians.

Now, there was about this time Jesus, a wise man, if it be lawful to call him a man...
Josephus Antiquities 18.63-64

... it would seem ridiculous to have a Jewish historian imply that Jesus was 'more than a man'... But ancient Christian forgers lived in their own world.
Authors

What Jewish literary witnesses are there to the existence of Jesus? The first to Jewish author who provides independent evidence for the first century existence of early Christianity is Flavius Josephus (ca 37 – ca 95 CE), a Jewish historian. As a general, he took part in the first war of Judea with Rome (66-70 CE) and after his capture by the Romans, became a favorite of the Roman general is later emperor, Vespasian. Four books by the Jewish historian are extant, his *Vita* (a brief autobiography), *The Jewish War*, *The Antiquities of the Jews*, and *Against Apion* (a defense of Jews). There are three passages in Josephus's *Antiquities* that refer either to Jesus, his brother James, or to John the Baptist. We will discuss only the first two here as we have discussed the passage of John the Baptist above.

Jewish References to Early Christians

James, the Brother of Jesus

After the death of the Roman procurator of Judea, and before the arrival of a new one, the high priest Ananus tried and executed some of his enemies. One of the victims, according to Josephus, was a man called James, "the brother of Jesus, who was called Christ..." (*Ant* 20.200). If the phrase "who was called Christ" is removed, no one would imagine that the James referred to was the brother of Jesus. Rather, one would have thought he was the brother of the high priest "Jesus, son of Damneus" (*Ant* 20.203) who is mentioned in the text only three sentences after the "Christ" phrase.

We regard this reference to Christ as a Christian interpolation. The use of the word *Christ* by Josephus also occurs in the Jesus passage at *Ant* 18.63-64. The only use of the word *Christians* appears there, too. Origen, more than 120 years later, is the first to refer to the passage about James (Celsus, I.47). Origen states that Josephus, "although not believing in Jesus as the Christ," attributes the destruction of Jerusalem and the Temple to the fact that "James the Just, who is the brother of Jesus (called Christ)..." was killed. The problem is that the extant manuscripts of Josephus do *not* say that the destruction of the Temple was a consequence of the death of James (cf. *Ant* 20.200-203).

Jesus, the Christ

The most famous passage used to demonstrate that Josephus had independent knowledge of the existence of Jesus appears in *Ant* 18.63-64:

> "Now, there was about this time Jesus, a wise man, *if it be lawful to call him a man*, for he was a doer of wonderful works... a teacher of such men as receive the truth with pleasure. He drew over to him both many of the Jews, and many of the Gentiles. *He was [the] Christ*; and when Pilate, at the suggestion of the principal men amongst us, had condemned him to the

cross, those that loved him at the first did not forsake him, *for he appeared to them alive again the third
day, as the divine prophets had foretold these and ten
thousand other wonderful things concerning him*; and
the tribe of Christians, so named from him, are not
extinct at this day." (Our italics identify those words
which many scholars find inauthentic.)

Some scholars believe this entire passage about Jesus the Christ
is a late Christian insertion. It breaks the flow of the narrative,
not relating to what comes before or what follows. Origen (ca 230
CE), who knew of Josephus's references to the stories of John the
Baptist and James, was not aware of this passage about Jesus.
This passage from *Antiquities* is unknown to any ancient writer
until the dishonest Eusebius[1] who wrote more than 200 years
after Josephus.

Would a Jewish historian, a defender of monotheism, write of
the man Jesus, "if it be lawful to call him a man?" And where
do Mark or the other Gospels say that many "Gentiles" were
attracted to Jesus during his ministry? Besides, why wasn't
Josephus a convert if he believed Jesus was (the) Christ and
more than a man? The answer is that some ancient Christians
believed that Josephus was a (secret) Christian; indeed some
thought he was Bishop of Jerusalem. The Christian who interpolated this passage thought that Josephus was a convert, and
thus he did not see the glowing description of Jesus ascribed to
Josephus as odd at all. Christian writings of the Imperial period
were often forged. Many forgeries survive to this day, for example, the *Protevangelium of James*, the *Acts of Pilate*, etc. Some,
like the *Shepherd of Hermas* and 1 Clement, nearly made it into
the canon of the *Christian Scriptures*.

Often a forged reference to Jesus was a glowing tribute, especially if the person was thought to be a secret Christian like Josephus, Philo of Alexandria, Pontius Pilate, Mrs. Pilate, Joseph of
Arimathea, or Nicodemus. To the modern reader it would seem
ridiculous to have a Jewish historian implied that Jesus was
"more than a man" in a book which supposedly concealed Jose-

---

[1]See Bauer, Walter, *Orthodoxy and Heresy in Earliest Christianity*, 2nd German ed., Trans. Paul J. Achtemeier, et al, Robert A. Kraft and Gerhard Krodel,
Eds. (Philadelphia: Fortress Press, 1971).

phus's conversion to Christianity. But ancient Christian forgers lived in their own world. As late as the 19th century CE, Christians like William Whiston, Josephus's translator, thought that Josephus was a Christian!

We conclude that these passages in Josephus's *Antiquities* are Christian interpolations. None of the other passages in Josephus contain any allusions to Christians. Shaye J. D. Cohen writes that Josephus "... can invent, exaggerate, over-emphasize, distort, suppressed, simplify, or, occasionally, tell the truth. Often we cannot determine where one practice ends and another begins."[2] Perhaps, but these remarks apply equally to certain ancient Christian editors.

Other Jewish Writings

Other Jewish documents of the first century CE will not detain us long in our search for independent witnesses to early Christians, since none of them mentioned Christians. Philo, the Alexandrian (ca 20 BCE-ca 50 CE), was a Jewish philosopher and biblical exegete. He lives in Alexandria, Egypt, and travel to Rome to present the grievances of Jews to the Emperor Caligula (39-40 CE). Philo thus had the opportunity to meet and comment on early Christians, but he knows nothing of the "famed" Christ or his followers.

Another first-century Jewish source is the Dead See Scrolls, more than 500 scrolls were found in caves near Qumran on the shores of the Dead Sea only about 20 miles from Jerusalem. The Qumranites lived at Qumran from circa 150 BCE to circa 68 CE. Married members of the sect apparently lived in Jerusalem and other cities.[3] There is no mention in the Scrolls of Jesus, John the Baptist, his disciples, or early Christians.

Many apocryphal books survive which were written by Jews between ca 200 BCE and 200 CE, like Tobit, Judith, 1 and 2 Maccabees, etc., and none of these mention Jesus or Christians. Sixty-five pseudepigrapha have been collected and published by

---

[2]Shaye J. D. Cohen (1979: 181) as quoted in Crossan, John Dominic, *The Historical Jesus: The Life of a Mediterranean Jewish Peasant* (San Francisco: Harper, 1991), 91.

[3]Most scholars today believe this sect to be the Essenes mentioned by Josephus and later Christian writers.

James H. Charlesworth in his two volume work, *The Old Testament Pseudepigrapha.* Many of these books were written in the same time period as the apocryphal books but, except for a few Christian interpolations, these works contain no allusions to Christians either.

Pagan References to Early Christians

This section examines the supposed early pagan literary references to Jesus. Epictetus (ca 60-ca 138 CE), a Stoic philosopher, uses the term "the Galileans" once (*Discourses*, IV.7). He may mean Christians, but in any case, his reference is too late. The Emperor Marcus Aurelius (121-180 CE), a Stoic philosopher, names "the Christians" once (*Meditations* 11.3). The allusion is late second century, and may be a gloss.

Galen

Galen, philosopher and physician (ca 130-ca 200), mentions the "followers of Moses and Christ" and "the school of Moses and Christ." He seems not to differentiate between the two "schools" of Judaism and Christianity.[4]

Lucian and Apuleius

Lucian, the Greek satirist, and Apuleius, author of the Roman novel, *The Golden Ass*, also mention the Christians,[5] but they are contemporaries of Galen, and their comments are too late to be considered. These references appear too late to give us independent verification of the existence of Jesus or early Christianity. No one after all denies that Christianity existed by the late first and early second centuries. This leaves three additional pagan references to examine, and one Christian reference.

---

[4]Wilken, Robert L., *The Christians as the Romans Saw Them* (New Haven: Yale University Press, 1984), 72-72.

[5]Wilken, R., 68.

Pliny and Trajan

In 111 CE, Pliny the Younger was appointed by his uncle, the Emperor Trajan, as governor of the province of Bithynia (in Asia Minor). One of his responsibilities was to investigate charges brought by local citizens against Christians. Pliny wrote a letter to the emperor (No 10.96) in 112 CE inquiring how he is to deal with Christians charged with crimes.[6] Pliny does not name the city involved. In the collection of sixty letters of Pliny, there is no other mention of Christians. Other than this letter, there is no evidence that would indicate that Pliny even knew of the existence of Christians.

Pliny does not indicate what crimes Christians were charged with, but we agree with R. Wilken that the letter of Pliny hints at cannibalism.[7] We also agree with him when he writes, "...that the accusations of promiscuity and ritual murder appear *only* in Christian authors. They are *not* present in the writings of pagan critics of Christianity."[8] (Wilken's ital.)

In seeking to find some evidence for Roman persecution of religion, Wilken dredges up the Bacchae of the second century BCE, some of whom were apparently repressed by the Roman state. He admits that those who practiced the rites of the Bacchanalia, if the rites were traditions of long standing, were exempt from persecution. He neglects to inform the reader that, according to Christian evidence, Christianity was still seen as a Jewish sect in the time of Pliny. For example, the references to Christians in Galen at the end of the second century CE refer to the Christians as "the school of Moses and Christ." Why then would Christianity not be exempted from persecution as was the ancient religion of Judaism?

Wilken admits the romanticized martyr tradition that accused Christians of cannibalism and so on, is from a later time, and so, "...cannot be simply read back into..." Pliny's situation.[9] But this is precisely what Wilken does.

Pliny had expected to find that Christians were guilty of crimes,

---

[6]Meier, John P., *A Marginal Jew: Rethinking the Historical Jesus Vol 1: The Roots of the Problem and the Person* (New York: Doubleday, 1991), 92.

[7]Wilken, R., 21.

[8]Ibid.

[9]Wilken, R., 21.

but states that he did not find them so. He writes that they "chant verses... in honor of Christ as if to a god...."[10] And what else do the Christians do? Well, of course, they "...bind themselves by oath,... to abstain from theft, robbery, and adultery...." Why then would Pliny execute them? He was conscientious enough to write the Emperor to make sure that he made no mistakes.

Even more "curious" is the fact that Pliny proceeds with his actions against the Christians without having received a reply from the emperor in this matter. Wilken admits that this is not characteristic of Pliny's character, which was one of "customary deliberateness."[11] Why would Pliny commit a criminal act by executing a person merely because they said they were Christian, when he knew that merely claiming to be a Christian was not a crime? The Christian god was not in the Roman Pantheon; this did not mean that Christianity was a criminal organization. True, Pliny adds something about Christians being obstinate and so should be punished, but obstinacy was not a crime under Roman law.

Finally, Pliny's letter tells us that some Christians claimed to be only *former* Christians, and so a test was given by Pliny. If these people, claiming to be former followers of Jesus, invoked the gods, offered wine and incense, and reviled the name of Christ, they would be let go. Wilken admits this tale of refusal to throw a bit of incense on the pagan altar is a later Christian tradition. So he goes looking for a Roman legal precedent, but fails to find a valid one.

After this letter regarding the Christians, Pliny's letters return to the subjects of his previous letters, which pertain to the governor's duties. Christians are never mentioned again.

Tacitus

Writing a few years after Pliny's letter of 112 CE, the historian, Tacitus (ca 56 CE-ca 117 CE), was the most blatant pagan anti-Semite of the ancient world that we know of. Around 64 CE, Nero, apparently looking for scapegoats, supposedly blamed

---

[10]quoted in Wilken, R., 22.
[11]Wilken, R., 22.

Christians for the burning of Rome. Of course, *Rome* was not burned. At most, Tacitus claims that some parts of the city were set afire. Modern historians think that the parts of Rome affected were the slum areas, the working class sections of the city. It is hard to see how Nero's palatial buildings could have had fire anywhere near them. In any case, he was out of the country.

Once again, we find the usual *trademarks* of the Christian forger. The Christian martyrs resemble those of the later centuries, gloriously accepting death. Their pagan persecutors are brutal monsters who feed their innocent victims to wild dogs. First, Nero slaughters admitted Christians, then a large number, not known to be Christians, are killed, mostly for "antisocial tendencies."[12] We find passages in the *Annals* of Tacitus which confirm some historical details of the gospels. He just happens to mention that "the Christ" was executed under Tiberius by Pontius Pilate, that Christianity originated in Judea, and early on arrived in Rome. Wilken characterizes Tacitus' history as "disinterested" testimony.[13]

The real reason for the popularity of the Tacitus witness is that the later Christians of the ancient world saw Nero as an "anti-Christ" who engaged in empire-wide persecution of Christians. Evidence has led modern apologists to lean more to blaming Domitian for a certain degree of persecution of Christians, as opposed to Nero. But apologists have held on to Nero as, at least, a local persecutor or Christians.

Suetonius

The last pagan source to be examined is *Lives of the Caesars* by Suetonius (ca 69 CE–ca 140 CE). His *Lives* was written a little later than Tacitus' *Annals*, in the first quarter of the second century. Writing in reference to Claudius (ca 49 CE), Suetonius states that the emperor "...banished the Jews from Rome, since they had made a commotion because of Chrestus."[14] Some scholars think this may be a reference to Jews being expelled

---

[12]Hoffman, R. Joseph, *Jesus Outside the Gospels* (New York: Prometheus Books, 1984), 60.

[13]Wilken, R., 149.

[14]quoted in Hoffman, R., 60.

from Rome (cf. Acts 18.2). It is not clear whether this reference is to Christians or to messianic Jews.

In the *Twelve Caesars*, writing of Nero's reign, Suetonius mentions in passing a "...'new and mischievous' sect..."[15] No mention is made of Jesus or Judea.

These preposterous stories of the lawless persecution of innocent Christians are not credible. Why would men of such prestigious offices and power be concerned with a small, innocuous sect, one of many floating around the Empire?

Muratorian Fragment

"The document [Muratorian fragment] is best regarded as a list of New Testament books recognized as authoritative in the Roman church at the time."[16] Bruce thinks the time the fragment was written is "...most probably to the end of the second century (CE)."[17] But then again F.F. Bruce seems to assume that Jesus walked around Palestine with a secretary who took shorthand. The Muratorian fragment is important since it is used to show that the Christians of the second century had the basic canon of the *Christian Scriptures*. But the fragment supplies no such evidence. *The Interpreter's Dictionary*, like Bruce and most modern writers, accepts a late second-century date for the Muratorian fragment.[18] However, in its Supplemental Volume, the *Dictionary* includes an article by A.C. Sundberg, Jr., which disputes the age of the Muratorian fragment.

Sundberg writes, "The early dating of the fragment has been based almost exclusively upon the phrase *nuperrime temporibus nostris*, usually translated 'very recently, in our time,' and taken to mean, within a generation of Pius I." (late 2nd cent).[19] Sundberg reminds us that such a phrase was used by ancient Christians in a way that "...could... mean 'most recently,' with respect to the previously named books; and 'in our time' could therefore

---

[15]Hoffman, R., 61.

[16]Bruce, F.F., *The Canon of Scripture* (Downers Grove, Il: InterVarsity Press, 1988), 159.

[17]Bruce, F.F., 158.

[18]*Interpreters Dictionary*, vol 1, 527.

[19]*Interpreters Dictionary*, Supp Vol, 610.

just as well refer to postapostolic times in general...."[20]

Sundberg writes, "This partial list of NT books, previously held to have originated in Rome about the end of the second century, must now probably be regarded as Eastern, dating from the early fourth century."[21]

The following is an abbreviated list of pagan writers who lived at the time of Jesus or within a century thereafter who do not mention Jesus or early Christians: Seneca, Pliny the Elder, Juvenal, Martial, Petronius, Plutarch, Epictetus, Lucian, Dio Chrysostom.[22]

[20] *Interpreters Dictionary*, Supp Vol, 610.

[21] *Interpreters Dictionary*, Supp Vol, 609.

[22] Remsberg, John E., *The Christ: A Critical Review and Analysis of the Evidence of His Existence* (Amherst: Prometheus Books. 18-19.

Appendix B

Second - Fourth Century

Perhaps the saddest thing to admit is that those who rejected the Cross have to carry it, while those who welcomed it so often engaged in crucifying others.
— Nicholai A. Berdyayev, *Christianity and Anti-Semitism*

The man who says to men, "Believe as I do, or God will damn you," will presently say, "Believe as I do, or I shall kill you."
— Voltaire, *Selected Works.*

The Lord said, "I will give you as a light to the nations, that my salvation may reach to the end of the earth."
— Isaiah 49.6

We decree and order that from now on, and for all time, Christians shall not eat or drink with Jews...
— Pope Eugenius IV Decree, 1442 CE

Second Century Christian Views on Judaism

The central problem with Christian scholarship on Judaism was best expressed by Samuel Sandmel, "It can be set down as something destined to endure eternally that the usual Christian commentators will disparage Judaism and its supposed legalism...." Sandmel concludes "...that with those Christians who persist in deluding themselves about Jewish legalism, no academic communication is possible. The issue is not to bring these interpreters to love Judaism, but only to bring them to a responsible, elementary comprehension of it."[1]

The Christian writers of the second century CE had no trouble understanding the central message of the *Christian Scriptures*, as can be seen in the writings of Ignatius, Justin Martyr, and Irenaeus.

R. Wilde writes that Bishop Ignatius (d ca 117 CE) saw Judaism as "...the old and bitter leaven, whereas Christianity is the new leaven."[2]

Justin Martyr (fl c 160 CE) says that the old covenant with the Jews has been replaced by the new covenant with the Christians.[3] Justin asserts that the "...Israel of God is no longer the Jewish nation but the Christians...."[4]

Irenaeus, Bishop of Lyons about 180 CE, asserts that the Christian God adopted "the gentiles" as his sons.[5] He believed that "the Jews" lapsed into idolatry and so are condemned.[6] The Law was given to Jews "...because of their stubbornness and because they would not subject themselves to Him,"[7] and because of "...their blindness."[8] Irenaeus writes that, as was prophesied in the Jewish Scriptures, "...the crucifixion of Christ was followed by the obliteration of..." the Jewish Law "...and the deliverance of the Jews into the hands of the Gentiles."[9] Thus "...they die in torment."[10]

Jews on Pagans

According to the *Jewish Scriptures*, can non-Jews be "saved?"

"I will give you as a light to the nations, that my salvation may reach to the end of the earth" (Isa 49.6; cf. Isa 2.2f, 56.6-8, and

---

[1]Sandmel, Samuel, *The First Christian Century*, 66, as quoted in E.P. Sanders, *Paul and Palestinian Judaism*, 1977, Minneapolis: Fortress Press, 1989, 35.

[2]Wilde, R., 85.

[3]Wilde, R., 108.

[4]Wilde, R., 109.

[5]*Demonstratio*, 8, as quoted in Wilde, R., 150.

[6]Wilde, R., 151.

[7]*Adv. Haer.*, 4:15,2; 4:16,4: in servitutem, as quoted in Wilde, R., 151.

[8]Ibid.

[9]*Adv. Haer*, 4:33,12, as referred to in Wilde, R., 153.

[10]*Demonstratio*, 69, as referred to in Wilde, R., 153.

45.22, all of which refer to the salvation of gentiles in general). Isa 66.19-20 predicts, as E. P. Sanders reminds us, a mission to save the gentiles.[11] The Jewish Scriptures never assert that righteous pagans are doomed. E.P. Sanders says that most Jews believed that righteous pagans would be saved.[12]

Persecution of Pagans and Jews by Christians in the 4th Century

Justin addresses emperor Antoninus Pius in his *First Apology*, and "argues for the unique validity of Christianity and claims that demons were responsible for pagan myths mimicking Christianity and for the scandalous allegations against Christians."[13] Justin condemns the followers of the Gnostic Christian, Marcion, as sexually permissive and cannibalistic.[14]

Justin's pupil, Tatian (ca 150), says the Greek religion and culture are stupid. He says he was once in the mysteries and that demons incited the evil in these mysteries.[15]

What did all this Christian intolerance lead to? If there is any doubt as to the exclusiveness of ancient Christianity, there can be no doubt once it attained power, i.e., was proclaimed the official state religion in the fourth century CE. Depriving Jews and pagans of their religious and civil rights was intense, widespread, and brutal. We shall give some examples. (For more details see *Paganism and Christianity* by Ramsay MacMullen and Eugene N. Lane (Chapter 22), and *The Death of Classical Paganism* by John Holland Smith.)

Theodore, the future Bishop of Mopsuestia (southern Turkey), in ca 380 abjures Satan and all his angels, i.e., poets, pagan philosophers, heretics, and those who believe in pagan purifications. His catechism says, "It is service of Satan that one should indulge in the observances of Judaism." It also condemns Christian heretics, the theater, the circus, contests of athletes, secular songs and dance "...which the devil introduced into this world

---

[11]Sanders, E.P., *Paul and Palestinian Judaism*, 1977 (Minneapolis: Fortress Press, 1989), 214.

[12]Ibid.

[13]Beard, M., *Religions of Rome*, 330 12.7a (i).

[14]Ibid.

[15]Beard, M., *Religions of Rome*, 331ff.

under the pretext of amusement... through which he leads the souls of men to perdition."[16]

Theodosian Code 4th Century and Later

What follows is from the chronological chart in J. H. Smith's book, *The Death of Classical Paganism.*[17]

The Edict of Toleration (311 CE) supposedly granted equality to all religions, but actually favored Christianity.

Between 318 CE and 789 CE, some of the laws passed by Christians included:

318 CE: "Converts from Judaism protected," but not vice versa.

340 CE: Paganism banned by Emperor Constans

379 CE: "Heretics outlawed in the East..."

381 CE: "Sacrifices at any shrine prohibited... conversion to paganism forbidden."

391 CE: "Private sacrifices forbidden."

397 CE: "All privileges stripped from continuing pagans."

398 CE: "All temples ordered destroyed."

408 CE: "Edicts banning heretics from public office in the East. Destruction of W(estern) temples ordered."

409 CE: "Astrologers banned by Honorius."

410 CE: "Paganism totally outlawed."

448 CE: The works of the most astute pagan critic of Christianity, Porphyry, were burned.

529 CE: The Christian Emperor Justinian closed the School of Athens.

609 CE: "The Pantheon dedicated as *Sancta Maria ad Martyres,....*" a Christian Church.

742-789 CE: New laws and ones reinforcing previous laws forbidding pagan practices.

Christians were forbidden to work for Jews as servants, and later could not employ Jews as servants. Jews were forbidden to be pupils of Christian teachers. Jewish conversion to Christianity was allowed, but the reverse was a capital offense. In-

---

[16]MacMullen and Lane, 279-280.

[17]Smith, John Holland, *The Death of Classical Paganism* (New York: Charles Scribner's Sons, 1976), 251-267.

termarriage between Jews and Christians was forbidden. Jews in general were required to pay for a Christian church if it were destroyed, allegedly by Jews, but when it was known that Christians destroyed a synagogue, Bishop Ambrose (ca 380 CE) successfully opposed compensation to Jews by Christians. Eventually, even Jewish religious teachings in the synagogue were required to have prior approval by Christian authorities.

The last pagan emperor, Julian "the Apostate" (ca 362-363 CE), though much slandered by the Christians, tried to restore religious freedom to the empire. He protested that Christian writers dishonored the gods which inspired Homer, Thucydides and others.

Jews are a small minority in the Christian-dominated Western world of today and the ancient pagans are not here to defend themselves. The thesis of our book can, of course, be rejected, but if scholars are ever to unveil the origins of one of the world's great religions, they will have to avoid pro-Christian bias, and prejudice against Jews and pagans.

* * *

Jn 8.32 Jesus said, "...and you will know the truth, and the truth will make you free."

Bibliography

All quotations from the Bible, unless otherwise stated, are from *New Revised Standard Version* (NRSV), Nashville: Thomas Nelson Publishers, 1990.

Balch, David L., Everett Ferguson, and Wayne A. Meeks, Eds. *Greeks, Romans, and Christians: Essays in Honor of Abraham J. Malherbe*. Minneapolis: Fortress Press. 1990.

Bauer, Walter. *Orthodoxy and Heresy in Earliest Christianity*. 2nd German ed., Trans. Paul J. Achtemeier, et al. Robert A. Kraft and Gerhard Krodel, Eds. Philadelphia: Fortress Press, 1971.

Beard, Mary, John North, and Simon Price, Eds. *Religions of Rome Volume 2: A Sourcebook*. Cambridge: Cambridge University Press, 1998.

Beck, Norman A. *Mature Christianity in the 21st Century: The Recognition and Repudiation of the Anti-Jewish Polemic of the New Testament*. Crossroad Publishing Co. 1994.

Borgen, Peder, and Soren Giversen, Eds. *The New Testament and Hellenistic Judaism*. Peabody, MA: Hendrickson Publishers, Inc., 1995.

Boring, M. Eugene, Klaus Berger, and Carsten Colpe, Eds. *Hellenistic Commentary to the New Testament* (HCNT). Nashville: Abingdon Press. 1995.

Brodie, Thomas L., *The Quest for the Origin of John's Gospel; A Source-Oriented Approach*. New York/Oxford: Oxford University Press, 1993.

Brown, Raymond E.. *The Death of the Messiah*. 2 vols. 1994. New York: Doubleday, 1998.

——. *The Gospel According to John*. 2 vols. 1966. The Anchor Bible. Garden City: Doubleday & Company, Inc., 1986.

——. *An Introduction to the New Testament*. New York: Doubleday & Company, Inc., 1997.

——. *New Testament Essays*. New York/Ramsey: Paulist Press, 1965.

Bruce, F.F. *The Canon of Scripture*. Downers Grove, Il: Inter-Varsity Press, 1988.

Bufe, Charles, Ed. *The Heretic's Handbook of Quotations: Cutting Comments on Burning Issues*. (expanded edition) Tucson, AZ: Sharp Press, 1992.

Bultmann, Rudolph. *The History of the Synoptic Tradition.* Trans. John Marsh. Peabody, MA: Hendrickson Publishers., 1963.

Cartlidge, David R., and David L. Dungan. *Documents for the Study of the Gospels.* Philadelphia: Fortress Press, 1980.

Charlesworth, James H. "From Messianology to Christology: Problems and Prospects." in Charlesworth, James H., Ed. *The Messiah: Developments in Earliest Judaism and Christianity.* Minneapolis: Fortress Press, 1992.

——. *Jesus' Jewishness: Exploring the Place of Jesus within Early Judaism.* New York: Crossroad, 1991.

——. *Jews and Christians: Exploring the Past, Present, and Future.* New York: Crossroad Publishing Co. 1990.

——. *The Messiah: Developments in Earliest Judaism and Christianity.* Minneapolis: Fortress Press, 1992.

Cohen, Shaye J. D., Ed. *From the Maccabees to the Mishnah.* 1987. Philadelphia: The Westminster Press, 1989.

Cohn-Sherbok, Dan. *A Dictionary of Judaism and Christianity.* Philadelphia: Trinity Press International, 1991.

Cohn-Sherbok, Lavinia and Dan. *A Popular Dictionary of Judaism.* (1995). Chicago: NTC Publishing Group, 1997.

Collins, Adela Yarbro. "Apotheosis and Resurrection." in Peder Borgen and Soren Giversen, Eds. *The New Testament and Hellenistic Judaism,* Peabody, MA: Hendrickson Publishers, Inc. 1995, 88-100.

Cotter, Wendy. *Miracles in Greco-Roman Antiquity : A Sourcebook.* Routledge. 1999.

Crossan, John Dominic. *The Historical Jesus: The Life of a Mediterranean Jewish Peasant.* San Francisco: Harper, 1991.

—, John Dominic. *Who Killed Jesus?* San Francisco: HarperSanFrancisco. 1995.

D'Angelo, Mary, "(Re)Presentations of Women in the Gospels: John and Mark" in Ross Shepard Kraemer and Mary Rose D'Angelo, Eds. *Women & Christian Origins.* New York: Oxford University Press, 1999.

Detering, Hermann. "The Dutch Radical Approach to the Pauline Epistles." *The Journal of Higher Criticism* 3 (Fall 1996): 163-193 [JHC].

Doherty, Earl. *The Jesus Puzzle: Did Christianity Begin with a Mythical Christ? Challenging the Existence of an Historical Jesus.*

Ottawa, Canada: Canadian Humanist Publications, 1999.

Doughty, Darrell J. "Pauline Paradigms and Pauline Authenticity." *The Journal of Higher Criticism* 1 (Fall 1994): 95-128.

Downing, F. Gerald. *Cynics, Paul and the Pauline Churches: Cynics and Christian Origins II*. New York: Routledge, 1998.

Epictetus. *Discourses of Epictetus, The: The Handbook, Fragments*. Robin Hard, Translator. London: Orion Publishing Group, 1995.

Feder, Lillian. *Apollo Handbook of Classical Literature*. 1964. New York: Thomas Y. Crowell Company, 1970.

Feldman, Louis H. *Jew & Gentile in the Ancient World*. Princeton, NJ: Princeton University Press, 1993.

Feldman, Louis H., and Meyer Reinhold, Eds. *Jewish Life and Thought Among Greeks and Romans*. Minneapolis: Fortress Press, 1996.

Ferguson, Everett. *Backgrounds of Early Christianity*. 1987. Grand Rapids: W. B. Eerdmans Publishing Co. 2nd Edition 1993.

Finegan, Jack. *Myth & Mystery: An Introduction to the Pagan Religions of the Biblical World*. Grand Rapids: Baker Book House, 1989.

Fitzmyer, Joseph A., S.J. *The Gospel According to Luke*. 2 vols. The Anchor Bible. New York: Doubleday, 1981.

Freedman, David Noel. Ed. in Chief. *The Anchor Bible Dictionary*. vol 5. New York: Doubleday, 1992.

Funk, Robert W., Ed. *The Acts of Jesus: The Search for the Authentic Deeds of Jesus*. Polebridge Press. 1998.

Griffiths, J. Gwyn. "Hellenistic Religions." 237-258 in *Religions of Antiquity*. Ed. Robert M. Seltzer.

Grimal, Pierre. *The Penguin Dictionary of Classical Mythology*. London: Penguin Books, 1991.

Haenchen, Ernst. *The Acts of the Apostles: A Commentary*. Trans. from the 14th German edition (1965), revised by R. McL. Wilson. Philadelphia: The Westminster Press, 1971.

Helms, Randel. *Gospel Fictions*. Buffalo: Prometheus Books, 1988.

Hengel, Martin. *Crucifixion*. Philadelphia: Fortress Press, SCM Press Ltd., London, 1977. Trans. from German ed. of 1976.

Hoffman, R. Joseph. *Jesus Outside the Gospels.* New York: Prometheus Books, 1984.

Interpreters Dictionary of the Bible, The: An Illustrated Encyclopedia. Nashville: Abingdon Press, 1962. 6 vols.

Kraemer, Ross Shepard and Mary Rose D'Angelo, Eds. *Women & Christian Origins.* New York: Oxford University Press, 1999.

Lachs, Samuel Tobias. *A Rabbinic Commentary on the New Testament: The Gospels of Matthew, Mark and Luke.* Hoboken, N.J.: KTAV Publishing House, Inc., 1987.

Ludemann, Gerd. *The Great Deception: And What Jesus Really Said and Did.* Prometheus Books. 1999.

Maccoby, Hyam. *Paul and Hellenism.* Philadelphia: Trinity Press International, 1991. Vallentine, Mitchell & Co., Ltd., 1963.

Mack, Burton L. *A Myth of Innocence; Mark and Christian Origins.* Philadelphia: Fortress Press, 1988, 1st paperback 1991.

MacMullen, Ramsay, and Eugene N. Lane, Eds. *Paganism and Christianity* 100-425 CE: A Sourcebook. Minneapolis: Fortress Press, 1992.

Martin, Francis. Ed. *Narrative Parallels to the New Testament.* Society of Biblical Literature. Atlanta: Scholars Press, 1988.

Martini, Cardinal Carlo Maria, "Christianity and Judaism: A Historical and Theological Overview." 19-34 in James H. Charlesworth, Ed. *Jews and Christians: Exploring the Past, Present, and Future.* New York: Crossroad Publishing Co. 1990.

Meier, John P. *A Marginal Jew: Rethinking the Historical Jesus Vol 1: The Roots of the Problem and the Person.* New York: Doubleday, 1991.

Metzger, Bruce M., Ed. *NRSV Exhaustive Concordance.* Nashville: Thomas Nelson Publishers, 1991.

Momigliano, Arnaldo, "Roman Religion of the Imperial Period," in *Religions of Antiquity,* Robert M. Seltzer, Ed., pp 218-236.

Motto, Anna Lydia. *Seneca.* New York: Twayne Publishers, Inc., 1973.

Neusner, Jacob. *The Mishnah: A New Translation.* New Haven and London: Yale University Press, 1988.

Philostratus. *The Life of Apollonius of Tyana.* Trans. F. C. Conybeare. Loeb Classical Library. Vol I. 1912. Harvard University Press, 1989.

Price, Robert M. "Apocryphal Apparitions: 1 Corinthians 15:3-11 as a Post-Pauline Interpolation." *The Journal of Higher Criticism* 1 (Fall 1995): 69-99.

Price, Robert M. *Deconstructing Jesus.* Amherst, NY: Prometheus Books, 2000.

Reale, Giovanni. Ed and Trans John R. Catan. *The History of Ancient Philosophy IV. The Schools of the Imperial Age.* State University of New York Press, 1990.

Roberts, Alexander, D.D., and James Donaldson, LL.D., Editors, *Ante-Nicene Fathers: Translations of The Writings of the Fathers down to A.D. 325* (ANF). American Reprint of the Edinburgh Edition. 10 vols. Grand Rapids: Wm. B. Eerdman's Publishing Company, Reprinted May 1987.

Remsberg, John E. *The Christ: A Critical Review and Analysis of the Evidence of His Existence.* Amherst: Prometheus Books. 1994.

Ruether, Rosemary Radford. *Faith and Fratricide: The Theological Roots of AntiSemitism.* 1974. New York: The Seabury Press, 1979.

Sanders, E.P. *The Historical Figure of Jesus.* Penguin USA. 1996.

——. *Jesus and Judaism.* 1985. Philadelphia: Fortress Press, 1989.

——. *Jewish Law from Jesus to the Mishnah.* Philadelphia: Trinity Press International, 1990.

——. *Paul and Palestinian Judaism.* 1977. Minneapolis: Fortress Press, 1989.

Sandmel, Samuel. *The First Christian Century in Judaism and Christianity: Certainties and Uncertainties.* New York: Oxford University Press, 1969.

Schweizer, Eduard. *The Good News According to Mark.* Atlanta: John Knox Press, 1970.

Schweizer, Eduard. *The Good News According to Matthew.* Westminster: John Knox Press, 1998.

Scholars Bible, The. Daryl D. Schmidt. Sonoma, CA: Polebridge Press, 1990.

Seldes, George, Ed., *The Great Thoughts.* New York: Ballantine Books, 1985.

Seltzer, Robert M. *Religions of Antiquity: Religion, History, and Culture.* New York: MacMillan Publishing Company. 1987, 1989.

Seneca. *Letters from a Stoic.* Selected and translated by Robin Campbell. London/New York: Penguin Books, 1969.

Smith, John Holland. *The Death of Classical Paganism.* New York: Charles Scribner's Sons, 1976.

Smith, Morton. *Jesus the Magician.* San Francisco: Harper, 1981 (1978).

Throckmorton, Jr., Burton H., Ed. *Gospel Parallels.* Nashville: Thomas Nelson Publishers, 1992.

Vermes, Geza. *Jesus the Jew: A Historian's Reading of the Gospels.* 1973. Philadelphia: Fortress Press, 1981.

Wansbrough, Henry, General Editor. *New Jerusalem Bible, The.* New York: Doubleday. 1990.

Wigoder, Geoffrey, Ed. in Chief. *Encyclopedia of Judaism, The.* New York: Macmillan Publishing Co., 1989.

Wikenhauser, Alfred. *New Testament Introduction.* Trans. J. Cunningham. Dublin, 1958, with many reprints.

Wilde, Robert. *The Treatment of the Jews in the Greek Christian Writers of the First Three Centuries.* Washington, D.C.: The Catholic University of America Press, 1949.

Wilken, Robert L. *The Christians as the Romans Saw Them.* New Haven: Yale University Press, 1984.

Winter, Paul. *On the Trial of Jesus.* Berlin: Walter de Gruyter and Son Co., 1961.

Made in the USA
Lexington, KY
12 August 2014